SOME OF THE REMARKABLE MEDICALLY-PROVEN BENEFITS OF ESSENTIAL FAT

WEIGHT LOSS

Essential fat helps burn excess calories instead of depositing them as fatty tissue. Easy weight loss is accomplished without strenuous dieting.

HEART DISEASE

Essential fat lowers serum cholesterol and tri-glycerides. It reduces the risk of thrombosis.

CANCER

Essential fat inhibits cancer cell growth.

DIABETES

Essential fat promotes more effective insulin utilization.

IMMUNE SYSTEM

Essential fat enhances the functioning of the T-suppressor lymphocytes that defend the body from invading bacteria and viruses.

(more!)

RHEUMATOID ARTHRITIS
Essential fat functions as an antiinflammatory catalyst.

PREMENSTRUAL SYNDROME
Essential fat alleviates 90 percent of PMS tensions and discomfort.

SKIN
Essential fat clears psoriasis, eczema, and acne.

NAILS
Essential fat hardens splitting, brittle nails.

CANDIDA ALBICANS
Essential fat controls yeast infections.

Beyond Pritikin

Ann Louise Gittleman, M.S.

with J. Maxwell Desgrey

BANTAM BOOKS

NEW YORK · TORONTO · LONDON · SYDNEY · AUCKLAND

NOTE

"Pritikin" is a registered trademark and service mark of Pritikin Programs, Inc. This book is neither sponsored by, endorsed by, nor associated with Pritikin Programs, Inc., or any of the Pritikin Longevity Centers.

BEYOND PRITIKIN

A Bantam Book
Bantam hardcover edition / April 1988
Bantam paperback edition / March 1989

Grateful acknowledgment is made for permission to reprint the following: Charts from the Nutrition Action Health letter, *copyright © 1985, Center for Science in the Public Interest. Excerpts from "Guess What's Coming To Dinner," copyright © 1987, Center for Science in the Public Interest. Excerpt from* Food Is Your Best Medicine *by Henry G. Bieler, M.D. Reprinted by permission of Random House, Inc.*

ISBN 0-553-27512-7

Published simultaneously in the United States and Canada

Bantam Books are published by Bantam Books, a division of Bantam Double-day Dell Publishing Group, Inc. Its trademark, consisting of the words "Bantam Books" and the portrayal of a rooster, is Registered in U.S. Patent and Trademark Office and in other countries. Marca Registrada. Bantam Books, 666 Fifth Avenue, New York, New York 10103.

PRINTED IN THE UNITED STATES OF AMERICA

OPM   14 13 12 11 10 9 8 7 6 5

This book is dedicated to
the memory of Harry Oliphant.

ACKNOWLEDGMENTS

My most sincere thanks to J. Maxwell Desgrey, whose vision and guidance provided the foundation for this book. To my literary agent, Michael Cohn, for believing in my project; Coleen O'Shea and Fran McCullough for their editorial guidance; Kris Dean for her expert typing and preparation of the manuscript; Steven Fowkes for his research assistance; Dr. Barry Sears for his technical expertise; and the late Wilma Keller for her loving spirit while I was working at the Pritikin Longevity Center; and thanks to all my understanding clientele who gave me support, encouragement, and the data that made this book possible.

A special expression of thanks is lovingly given to my dear personal friend and mentor, Lena Falcidia. Lena's prophetic wisdom and unflagging confidence in my writing abilities have finally come to fruition. Bless you, Lena.

CONTENTS

Foreword by Dr. Lendon Smith • xv
Introduction: My Pritikin Path • xix

1/ **Extending the Pritikin Prescription** • 1

The Heart of the Matter • 2
Omega-3 and Omega-6 • 3
How Omega-3 and Omega-6 Work:
   The Prostaglandins • 4
The Essential Fats • 5
The Essential Fat Solution • 5
Looking Forward • 8

2/ **Pritikin Promises and Pitfalls** • 9

The Diet/Disease Connection • 10
The Downside of the Pritikin Prescription • 11
Dietary Imbalances: Gluten Sensitivities
   and *Candida Albicans* • 11
New Findings: It's in the Fat • 14
Eat Fat and Lose Weight • 16
The Fat to Keep You Thin • 17
The Solution • 18

3/ **All About Essential Fats** • 23

Basic Fat Groups • 24
How Fats Work in the Body • 26
The Infamous Four • 27
The Heat Factor • 28
The Hydrogenation Factor • 28
The Oxygen Factor • 29
The Homogenization Factor • 30

4/ The New Nutrition Diet Weight Loss Connection • 33

Brown Fat • 35
The Big Picture • 37

5/ The New Nutrition Diet Prostaglandin Protection • 41

The Benefits of Prostaglandins • 44

6/ Polyunsaturates: Good Fats Gone Bad • 47

What Are the Essential Fats? • 49
Margarine: From Bad to Worse • 50

7/ The Monounsaturates and Saturates Among Us • 55

The Monounsaturates • 55
Enter Canola Oil • 56
The Saturates • 57
Fast Foods • 58
Convenience Foods • 59
Is There a Solution? • 60

8/ Cholesterol and the New Nutrition Diet • 63

High-Density Lipoproteins (HDL) and
  Low-Density Lipoproteins (LDL) • 65
Triglycerides • 71

9/ The New Nutrition Diet Food Choices: Where the Essential Fats Are Found • 73

The GLA Fat Burners • 74
Omega-3s • 75
Essential Fat Dietary Supplements • 76
Caveat Emptor: What the Buyer Should Know
  About Fish Oil Capsules • 77

Additional Fat Fighters • 78
Cell Defense • 79
Garlic and Onions • 80

10/ The Lowdown on Fiber • 83

11/ New Light on Fitness • 89

12/ Chemistry in the Kitchen • 93

Prime Contenders • 93
Prime Offenders • 95
Nutritional Bombshells • 96
The Life in Your Food • 97
Food Follies • 97
Nutritional Savvy • 98
Temperature Control • 99
Other Helpful Hints • 101
Selection of Vegetables and Fruits • 101
Successful Vegetable Storage • 102
Successful Fruit Storage • 103
Vegetable Preparation and Cooking • 103
Fruit Preparation and Cooking • 104
Fish, Fowl and Meat • 105
Successful Meat Storage • 105
Help Line • 106
Shellfish • 106
Seeds, Peanuts, Nuts, Beans, Egg Whites and
    Potatoes • 106
Desirable Cooking Methods • 107
Undesirable Cooking Methods • 109
Essential Utensils • 110
Essential Utensil Alert • 111

13/ The New Nutrition Diet Master Strategy • 115

Finding Fat • 115
Shaking Salt • 116
The Yeast Problem:
    The Twentieth Century Epidemic • 116

Sweet Surrender • 117
Where to Shop • 117
Before You Take a Bite • 118
Food Combinations • 119
Stocking and Storing the Staples • 120
A Cleansing Formula • 128
Mail Order Suppliers of Organic Food • 130
A Note About Irradiated Food • 137

14/ About the Diet: Questions and Answers • 139

The Ten-Point Prescription • 147

15/ The Two-Week Fat Flush • 149

Give Your Liver a Vacation • 150
The Fat Flush Program • 150
Detox While Dieting • 152
The Water Connection • 153
Putting It All Together • 154
Seasonal Tune-up • 156

16/ The New Nutrition Diet Prescription • 157

The New Nutrition Master Formula • 157
21-Day Master Menu Plan • 159
Recipes:
  Salad Dressings and Sauces • 169
  Pâtés • 174
  Soups • 176
  Main Events • 179
  Vegetables • 189
  Sweet Delights • 194
  Nouvelle Puddings • 197
  Fruit Gelatins • 199
  Fresh Fruit Sorbets • 200
  Grain Creations • 201
  Food Equivalents • 202
  Ten Transitional Tips • 208

17/ Spices and Herbs of Life • 211

Herbal Magic • 211
Seasoning Savvy • 212
Spice It Up • 214

18/ Eating Out Smart • 215

Appendix/Nutrition Education Resources • 221
References • 225
Index • 231
Recipe Index • 243

FOREWORD

In January 1985, an intriguing article appeared in the *New England Journal of Medicine* about the diet of our ancestors. According to the findings of the researchers, our ancestors of 1 to 20 million years ago ate a diet composed primarily of raw vegetables and raw low-fat meats. They did not have grains such as wheat, oats, and barley—food products which are found in contemporary high-fiber diets. Instead, they ate nuts and seeds when they found them and ate fruit only in season, as there was no way to preserve foods. And no dairy products were available (it's tough to milk a rhino on the run).

The researchers pointed out that our inherited digestive systems are adapted to the limited low-fat diets of our ancestors. It is also interesting to note that the meat in early man's diet contained less than 4 percent fat. This is an important fact which coincides with what we heard first from Nathan Pritikin: *cardiac risks are greatly increased by the American high-fat diet.* The good news from Pritikin was that cardiac risk factors can be reversed with low-fat intake.

The landmark *NEJM* article went on to state that the type of fat contained in the meats our ancestors ate was high in a special kind of fat called Omega-3, a crucial observation which coincides with the latest research into why the extremely high-fat Eskimo diet rich in Omega-3 fats *does not* clog arteries. Conversely, the meats which we Americans eat are low in Omega-3 fats yet high in Omega-6 fats, which tend to be more inflammatory, and we suffer from an astoundingly high incidence of heart disease. Researchers began to ask whether the *kind* of fat you eat isn't more important than the amount of fat you eat.

This book contains important information about the role of fats in our health. You may be surprised by some of what you read: for example, did you know that *dietary fat can actually help you lose weight?* The research on which this book is based is new and exciting. Ann Louise Gittleman has made a quantum leap beyond the Pritikin program, which was the first to make the public aware of the relationship of fats to diet and health, by integrating her valuable research with the beneficial lessons learned from her experience at the Pritikin Center.

Pritikin was an engineer, not an M.D. During his lifetime his work received no support from the American Heart Association. But after his death, his ideas were vindicated: the autopsy showed his blood vessels were as "clean as a preadolescent's." Twenty-eight years earlier, he had been told that his vessels were hopelessly sludged up and to get his will notarized. Engineers know how to do things. Pritikin did it.

Almost all of us have heard of the great benefits many cardiac-risk patients have experienced by spending two to four weeks at his Pritikin Longevity Centers. His program featured a low-fat diet and routine exercise to tolerance. By following this regime, people avoided the bypass operations which their general M.D.s had recommended. However, although the benefits were real and the patients felt better, there were some negative responses as well. Some were unhappy; some were hungry all the time. There may have been poor mineral absorption. Some patients developed arthritis, and some eczema appeared. What was going on? What was missing?

Now we have some answers—authoritative answers. Ann Louise Gittleman was there at the Pritikin Center watching history being made. She saw the obvious benefits of the ground-breaking Pritikin Nutrition Program, but after a while she began to see some evidence of new problems—problems that could only be attributed to the very low-fat, high-fiber diets, that Pritikin followers were consuming.

She discovered that we don't need lots of fat, but we absolutely must have certain fats, what Ann Louise calls essential fats, the cornerstone of what she calls the New Nutrition Diet. We cannot be Eskimos or Greenlanders, but we can learn from and imitate their fat intake. *The essential fats are not only the beneficial ones found in the Eskimo marine oils, the Omega-3 fats, but the ones found in unprocessed vegetable oils.* We know that these two sources of essential fat are more likely to lead to the good prostaglandins that regulate cellular function and protect against heart disease. Essential fats will probably save more lives than any of us realize.

Ann Louise is to be congratulated for sticking to her investigations until she found the reasons for the results the Pritikin diet was getting, the good and the negative. Everyone should read *Beyond Pritikin*, even doctors, who are supposed to know everything.

LENDON SMITH, M.D.

INTRODUCTION

MY PRITIKIN PATH

As fate would have it, my path to Pritikin began around the dinner table in September of 1980. I was at a family gathering where my uncle Jack, a pharmacist, asked for my help in locating hoop cheese and apple butter for a special diet plan. Knowing how conservative and traditional Jack was, I was surprised and intrigued by his interest in these unusual foods. When I questioned him, he told me he had placed himself on the Pritikin diet to help balance his blood sugar, and he was having excellent results controlling his adult-onset diabetes. He felt better than he had felt in the previous twenty years.

I was familiar with the diet because several years earlier I had read Nathan Pritikin's first book, *Live Longer Now*, written in 1974. I was impressed with the positive results Pritikin reported that his diet and exercise plan had on the management of coronary disease. At that time I was staff nutritionist at a health-care facility in Connecticut. It was ironic that Jack's inquiry would rekindle my interest in the diet/disease connection and ultimately lead me from Connecticut to California, where I would begin working with Nathan Pritikin.

After rereading *Live Longer Now*, I compiled a new resumé and sent it off to California in hopes of affiliating with the Pritikin organization. In less than a week I received a call from the Center's personnel director, who wanted to arrange an interview with me. In October 1980 I flew to Los Angeles and two months later became the Director of Nutrition at the main Pritikin Longevity Center in Santa Monica (another branch was located in North Miami, Florida).

As the Director of Nutrition at the Pritikin Center, I was very much a part of the growing self-help health movement that was sweeping the country. My formal education was basic and traditional: After receiving an undergraduate degree in English from Connecticut College in New London, I later enrolled in the New York Institute of Dietetics as part of the Dietetic Technician Program. After completing the institute's courses in menu planning, human physiology, nutritional pathology, biochemistry, microbiology, food sanitation, restaurant operation, and therapeutic nutrition, I went on to receive a master's degree in nutrition from Columbia University. Both the New York Institute of Dietetics and Columbia offered extensive field-work experience in local hospitals, where I observed food service activity, patients' food-tray preparation, and actively took part in dietary counseling. My first position after receiving my master's degree was chief nutritionist of the pediatric clinic at Bellevue Hospital in New York City. I later served as a bilingual nutritionist for the USDA's Women, Infants, and Children Food Program (WIC) at Hill Health Center in New Haven, Connecticut.

Besides my academic nutrition courses and experience, an important part of my education was studying and working with nutritionally oriented medical practitioners in the Connecticut area. In 1979 I became the staff nutritionist with Deepbrook Associates in Newtown, Connecticut, a progressive group of health-care professionals. Reading everything available on health, from clinical journals to health-food-store booklets, broadened my views on both traditional and alternative approaches to health. With my conventional background as a foundation for healthy skepticism, my mind was open to alternatives that worked.

As I more and more saw the need to educate the public in self-care and to make the diet/health connection integrated as a practical part of busy lifestyles, I lectured widely and appeared on radio and television.

My appointment as the Director of Nutrition at the Pritikin Longevity Center seemed a challenge worthy of focusing all my prior education, experience, and creativity. The Pritikin Center proved to be a refreshing professional and personal change. After three years in the public health field, I was growing frustrated with the apathy toward change regarding the highly saturated fat, high sugar, and low fiber content of the hospital and federal food programs. In contrast, developing and coordinating the entire nutrition education program at the Center was challenging and demanding. I enjoyed teaching people how to alleviate their diet-related health problems, specifically heart disease, diabetes, and circulatory disorders. Because taking personal responsibility was a primary tenet of the Pritikin principles, my audience was receptive and eager at my lectures. Our patients, or the "participants" as we called them, couldn't get enough information, restaurant tips, and recipe ideas. Optimism was generated from the experience of being a "participant" in one's health rather than a passive observer or victim.

And, too, Nathan Pritikin was always gracious and helpful. I will always remember the special favor he did for me soon after I arrived, when he rearranged a busy East Coast touring schedule to give a health lecture at my mother's women's group. Her organization recorded their largest turnout and Pritikin was acknowledged by a long standing ovation.

In 1982 I resigned my position as Director of Nutrition to pursue a wider field of clinical and research interests regarding the underlying causes of degenerative illness. The diet/disease connection was just beginning to explode. There was a whole new world of research findings, which were coming to light about essential fatty acids, food allergies, and *Candida albicans* (an increasingly prevalent yeast infection) that raised nutritional concerns not covered by the Pritikin prescription.

After leaving the Center I met J. Maxwell Desgrey, who further expanded my knowledge about nutrition. He had a deep interest in and knowledge of anti-aging and life-extension techniques both here and abroad. Through Jack I was introduced to alternative healing therapies such as fasting, detoxification, and full-spectrum light. He shared his personal experiences and volumes of research. Before resuming my private nutritional practice once again, we traveled together to visit state-of-the-art health programs throughout the world. Jack's journalism skills and investigative research have been invaluable in consolidating our findings.

Thus, *Beyond Pritikin* came full circle again five years later at a dinner table one evening in the New York Friars Club. I was the guest of a former Pritikin patient, clothing manufacturer Harry Oliphant, and his wife, Ann. After hearing of all the new information I had been gathering over the years, Harry said to me, "You've gone beyond Pritikin. You've got to write your book now." So I did, and here it is.

1

EXTENDING THE PRITIKIN PRESCRIPTION

Health is a journey, not a destination.
—ANONYMOUS

The Pritikin prescription for optimum health is a low-fat, low-cholesterol, low-sodium, high-complex-carbohydrate diet combined with regular aerobic exercise. In caloric percentages, Pritikin's diet is composed of 5 to 10 percent fat, 10 to 15 percent protein, and 80 percent complex carbohydrate. It consists of whole grains, beans, vegetables, fruits, nonfat dairy products, and small amounts of protein from beef, fowl, and fish. Protein consumption is limited to a lean 3.5 ounces a day in order to reduce total fat and cholesterol intake because most animal protein foods have high levels of fat and cholesterol.

Clearly a spartan diet, the Pritikin diet was successful in getting people off fat, salt, sugar, alcohol, coffee, and tobacco. It provided a firm foundation for sound and healthy eating habits. It promoted whole foods and regular daily exercise. In many cases the supervised program reduced blood pressure levels, decreased cholesterol levels, and greatly diminished insulin use by diabetics.

Although not a medical doctor, Pritikin was an avid medical researcher. His particular interest was coronary heart disease, because in 1955 he was diagnosed as suffering from a severe heart condition. Convinced that there was a correlation between diet and health, for over twenty-five years Pritikin researched medical literature on the degenerative diseases of the Western world such as cardiovascular disease, high blood pressure, diabetes, and cancer. He also studied the dietary patterns and lifestyles of societies which had much lower rates of degenerative illness. Pritikin then modeled his diet after the basic high-starch (complex carbohydrate) and low-fat food patterns of primitive cultures such as the Tarahumara Indians of northwestern Mexico, the Bantus of South Africa, and the natives of New Guinea.

The Heart of the Matter

The heart of the Pritikin diet is its extremely low fat content. He based his low-fat emphasis on his research findings that high-fat, high-cholesterol diets are linked with degenerative disease in the developed nations. Medical literature suggests that saturated fat can raise serum cholesterol levels, and that serum cholesterol is a key factor in the incidence of heart disease—the nation's Number One killer. Pritikin, however, restricted not only the saturated fats (which usually come from meat and full-fat dairy products) but banned all fats, including the unsaturated fats from vegetable, nut, and seed sources. Pritikin didn't acknowledge the beneficial value of any fats in the diet.

Pritikin's review of diets from all over the world, obviously prejudiced by his personal health concern, focused on the therapeutic cardiovascular aspects. Yet his investigations missed crucial evidence about the role of fat in the diet.

Omega-3 and Omega-6

Pritikin's research somehow overlooked the revolutionary fat insights of researchers H. O. Bang and John Dyerberg presented in a 1978 study published in *Lancet*, the highly respected British medical journal. Drs. Bang and Dyerberg investigated the diet of native Greenland Eskimos. They reported that despite an extremely high-fat, high-cholesterol diet, the Eskimos have a very low incidence of coronary heart disease, diabetes, and cancer. The connection between the Eskimos' high-fish diet and their low heart disease rate was suspected as early as 1855. These early population studies resurfaced with the Bang and Dyerberg observations of the 1970s.

It was reported that the traditional Eskimo diet contains over 70 percent of its calories in fat, and yet the Eskimos are free of killer degenerative illness such as heart disease. This figure represents a far cry from the recommended 10 percent of fat calories suggested by Nathan Pritikin to prevent and control disease. Despite this important new information published in 1978, Pritikin writes in his 1979 book *The Pritikin Program for Diet and Exercise*, "We feel that fats are so bad for you that you should eat no more than 5 to 10 percent fat."

The key to the Eskimos' excellent health is the kind of fat they eat. Eskimos get their fat from marine life (seal, whale, walrus) and fatty cold-water fish (herring, mackeral and salmon) that make up most of their diet. These foods contain marine oils which are high in two important Omega-3 fatty acids called eicosapentaenoic acid, or EPA, and docosahexaenoic acid, or DHA. *Omega-3 fatty acids in the form of EPA and DHA have been shown to protect the cardiovascular system.*

Another acknowledged leader in fat research, Dr. David Horrobin, began publishing in the early 1980s. Horrobin reported outstanding health results with another kind of fat, evening primrose oil, which contains substantial amounts of an Omega-6 fatty acid called gamma linolenic acid, or GLA. He showed that GLA helped cardiovascular problems, weight loss, inflammatory diseases such as arthritis, disorders of the immune system, alcoholism, premenstrual syndrome, and skin, hair, and nail conditions.

In fact, as early as the 1970s Hoffman-LaRoche published clinical data that showed the positive effects of adding fat in the form of GLA to the diet.

How Omega-3 and Omega-6 Work: The Prostaglandins

Both the Omega-3 and Omega-6 fatty acids work in the body by forming hormonelike substances called prostaglandins. The role of prostaglandins is to control the human body's daily function. As an indication of how important prostaglandins are, it is interesting to note that prostaglandin researchers were awarded three Nobel Prizes in medicine in 1982.

Prostaglandins control *all* body functions at the cellular level. They are vital in regulating the cardiovascular, reproductive, immune, and central nervous systems. Prostaglandins are needed to control clotting, inflammation, tumor growth, and allergies. The onset of disease is the result of a prostaglandin imbalance.

Prostaglandins protect against heart disease by:

- Making the blood thinner, less sticky, and less likely to clot
- Reducing platelet clumping
- Lessening constriction of the blood vessels

However, without certain fats in the diet, prostaglandins cannot perform their crucial and varied regulatory functions in the body.

The Essential Fats

There are two major types of essential fats: Omega-3 oils from fish and marine life, and Omega-6 oils from plant and botanical sources such as unrefined vegetable oils, borage, and evening primrose oil. These two families of essential fatty acids perform two major roles: (1) they form the cell membrane that surrounds every cell in the body, and (2) they are the source of prostaglandins, which have far-reaching regulatory effects throughout the human body.

Now is the time to reinstate essential fats into our diet because of these reasons:

- The decade long influence of the Pritikin Diet with its exclusion of all fats including healthful fats;
- Dietary trends toward eating fast foods in which the cooking process may make the fats harmful to the body; and,
- Misinformation about how indispensable the right fats are for total health.

The Essential Fat Solution

Essential fats are a fundamental component of what I call my New Nutrition Diet. The Essential Fat Solution is based on three crucial points:

1. Essential fat is fat that is absolutely necessary for the regulation of every function in the human body.

2. Essential fat is fat that must be included in the diet because it cannot be manufactured by the body.

3. Essential fat is fat that has not been nutritionally altered from its natural state by food processing or faulty cooking practices, yet has been purified of oil-soluble pesticides and herbicide residue.

New uses of essential fat are reported almost daily from around the world. For example, a study published in the *New England Journal of Medicine* in March 1986 indicated that *oils like olive and peanut oil are as effective in lowering cholesterol levels as a low-fat, high-carbohydrate diet.* The Greek island of Crete has the highest olive oil consumption in the world, and also the lowest mortality rate due to cardiovascular disease. Olive oil has been a staple in the Mediterranean countries for five thousand years. Despite this important information, there has been no change in the basic Pritikin prescription, and the ban on all fats is still the bottom line of the Pritikin diet.

Believe it or not, almost 80 million Americans are too fat and yet fat deficient. Sounds like a contradiction, doesn't it? It is even more of a contradiction when you consider that over 40 percent of the calories in the standard American diet comes from fat.

The right kind and the right amount of fat—the kind I call essential fat—will allow you to lose weight effortlessly and painlessly without becoming preoccupied with dieting. Essential fat is the healthiest and easiest way to attain and maintain your normal weight.

Obesity is only one of our national health problems that may be caused by lack of essential fat in the diet. As you will experience, essential fat is not only good for your waistline, it offers protection from many of the diseases that befall modern man. According to the studies of prominent fat researchers like Drs. William Connor, Donald Rudin, David Horrobin, and Barry Sears, essential fat (from EPA-containing fish oils, and GLA-containing vegetable and botanical oils) has proven effective in controlling, preventing, and reversing a number of disease conditions.

Essential fat benefits:

WEIGHT LOSS

Essential fat helps burn excess calories instead of depositing them as fatty tissue. Easy weight loss is accomplished without strenuous dieting.

HEART DISEASE

Essential fat lowers serum cholesterol and triglycerides. It reduces the risk of thrombosis.

CANCER

Essential fat inhibits cancer cell growth.

DIABETES

Essential fat promotes more effective insulin utilization.

RHEUMATOID ARTHRITIS

Essential fat functions as an antiinflammatory catalyst.

PREMENSTRUAL SYNDROME

Essential fat alleviates 90 percent of PMS tensions and discomfort.

IMMUNE SYSTEM

Essential fat enhances the functioning of the T-suppressor lymphocytes that defend the body from invading bacteria and viruses.

SKIN

Essential fat clears psoriasis, eczema, and acne.

NAILS

Essential fat hardens splitting, brittle nails.

CANDIDA ALBICANS

Essential fat controls yeast infections.

Looking Forward

Nathan Pritikin recognized that the standard American diet encouraged excessive intake of fat, but he did not distinguish between healthful fat and unhealthful fat and so excluded them all, including the fats from the Omega-3 and Omega-6 families, which are now recognized as absolutely crucial for health. Pritikin's program, which called for eliminating nuts, seeds, unrefined vegetable oils, fatty acid supplements, and fatty fish, excluded the most vital essential fat sources and the fat-soluble vitamins A and E from the diet.

Beyond Pritikin is about looking forward and extending the basic foundation of the Pritikin diet to a diet that includes essential fat—a life-supporting, lifelong eating plan based on state-of-the-art nutritional findings. That's why I call my program the New Nutrition Diet. And since people eat food, not nutrition, my diet is based on a return to the pleasures of eating seasonally fresh, wholesome foods. Finally, understanding that certain fats can be good for you is a boon to the health-conscious cook and consumer. Fat goes a long way in making food more palatable because it is such a potent flavor carrier and enhancer. And as an added benefit to the weight-conscious reader, this eating program will also help you lose weight.

2

PRITIKIN PROMISES AND PITFALLS

*Most maladies that afflict humanity
result from bad food or excess of
food that may even have been wholesome.*
—MAIMONIDES, THIRTEENTH CENTURY

The year 1985 marked the end of the low-fat era and gave birth to the philosophy that is the basis of the New Nutrition Diet. It was the year that Nathan Pritikin, the champion of the fat-free diet, died. It was also the year in which three landmark studies were published in the prestigious *New England Journal of Medicine.* These studies, from the Harvard Medical School, the Oregon Health Sciences University, and the University of Leiden in the Netherlands, correlated fish and the oil (fat) contained in fish with reducing cardiovascular disease and possibly rheumatoid arthritis and asthma as well.

Pritikin himself was the herald for a new age in the 1970s and early '80s which captured the attention of the American public. He advocated self-health in the form of diet and exercise. More than any other diet spokesman, he represented the fitness spirit of the times. The Pritikin Longevity Centers pioneered the burgeoning health consciousness and paved the way for the new breed of medical spas and preventive health centers that exist throughout the country today.

The Diet/Disease Connection

Pritikin's 1974 book, *Live Longer Now*, provided the model in the years that followed for a whole series of government reports on dietary recommendations. His low-fat, high-complex-carbohydrate message was echoed in the 1977 *Dietary Goals for the United States* issued by the Senate Select Committee on Nutrition and Human Needs. Then, in 1979, came the *Surgeon General's Report on Health Promotion and Disease Prevention*, which said: *"You the individual can do more for your own health and well-being than any doctor, any hospital, any drug, any exotic medical advice."*

This simple yet significant statement from the U.S. Surgeon General represented a major step forward in the attitude of traditional medical practices. It shifted the responsibility for health from doctors, drugs, and surgery to the individual. The Pritikin program epitomized this self-care attitude from the beginning.

A final accolade to the Pritikin principles came in 1982, when the National Academy of Sciences published a major report which, for the first time, associated dietary patterns with certain forms of cancer. At long last, medical evidence had linked another killer disease, cancer, to diet. Health had become a personal responsibility, requiring lifestyle and dietary changes. Now those who were ready to take this responsibility were hungry for "diet" information.

At the Pritikin Center where I was Director of Nutrition, I witnessed dramatic improvements in many participants who followed Pritikin's diet and whose case histories later became the statistics supporting the Pritikin program. Every day I scanned medical charts and reviewed blood values that demonstrated Pritikin's claim that "cholesterol was lowered on the average a full 24 percent and that over 50 percent of the adult-onset diabetics leave virtually free of insulin and after two weeks most hypertensives leave drug-free with lowered blood pressure."

The Downside of the Pritikin Prescription

Slowly, however, I began to experience the downside of the Pritikin experience. Even though the participants at the Center demonstrated many positive changes while staying there, some complained of problems after leaving, or when they returned for refresher courses. There were complaints about weight gain, feeling hungry all the time no matter how much food was eaten, and problems because of the inordinate amount of time needed to prepare and eat six to eight small meals a day. I also noticed a rather curious phenomenon among those participants who were on the program from one to two years—the appearance of vertical ridges on the fingernails, a syndrome that signals a nutritional deficiency.

Dietary Imbalances: Gluten Sensitivities and *Candida Albicans*

I began to wonder about the potential shortcomings of the Pritikin program. Pritikin studied the diet of the Tarahumara Indians of northwestern Mexico as a model for his low-fat, high-starch regimen. The Tarahumaras are recognized as the greatest long-distance runners in the world. Their diet features corn as the staple, while a major emphasis in the Pritikin plan is on whole grains. While both corn and grains are classified as complex carbohydrates, they differ in one major respect: *Grains such as wheat, rye, oats, and barley contain a substance called gluten, to which many individuals are sensitive.*

It used to be thought that gluten intolerance, also called celiac or sprue disease, was a relatively rare occurrence affecting only a small number of people. But recent findings show that more and more people are unable to assimilate wheat and similar grains because of excessive consumption of these foods. What we are now seeing is that the minority is becoming a majority with minor gluten malabsorption. When the high-carbohydrate diets came in style, many individuals became over-enthusiastic with the amounts of whole grains they added to their diet. Grains for breakfast in the form of cereal, then in sandwiches for lunch, in pasta for dinner, and in whole-grain cookies and muffins for snacks, created a metabolic overload.

Gluten is the protein portion of the grain that gives dough its elastic consistency. When gluten-rich grains are eaten in excess, persistent intestinal gas, bloating, irregular bowel movements, and fatigue can occur. Diarrhea, anemia, pallor, and mental instability can be created by gluten intolerance.

There is a growing number of people who suffer from minor gluten malabsorption. They are not aware that their digestive problems and lack of energy are caused by their excessively grain-rich diet.

Gluten intolerance has been linked to a number of disease conditions, such as multiple sclerosis, schizophrenia, arthritis, and autism. In adults, a kind of itching eczema characterized by small red bumps has been linked to gluten intolerance. This protein-containing substance found in grains impairs the intestinal lining and interferes with nutrient absorption. When the intestinal tract is diseased or damaged, the B vitamins—especially folic acid and B-12—are not well absorbed. Such deficiencies can result in classical anemia as well as mental confusion in addition to the primary gluten intolerance. Often vitamins or even vitamin injections are necessary to replace lost nutrients due to malabsorption.

The high fiber content of gluten-rich grains tends to carry minerals *out* of the body before they can be absorbed. Calcium, folic acid, and iron are often deficient in a heavy grain diet, as well as fat-soluble vitamins A and E. These combined vitamin and mineral deficiencies can create irregular menstrual cycles, vague aches and pains in the bones, and perhaps the ridged fingernail condition. Although the Pritikin diet is often referred to as the Caveman's Diet, the cavemen didn't eat grains. Cavemen relied on meats, vegetables, beans, fruits, berries, and nuts.

Which grains are gluten-free? Millet, corn, rice, quinoa, amaranth, and buckwheat. Flours made from arrowroot, tapioca, potatoes, and soybeans are good wheat-flour substitutes. But restricting grain from the diet may not be the only dietary change that needs to be made. Often a lactose intolerance accompanies the inability to digest gluten. So, avoiding milk is in order. Milk products like cheese and yogurt can usually be tolerated.

The various restrictions of the Pritikin diet promoted the overuse not only of grains but of yeast-related foods. These include fermented foods such as soy sauce and oil-free vinegar dressings, mushrooms (from the fungus family), and yeast-containing breads and crackers. Tomato sauce, a popular element in the diet, is also yeast-related because its processing creates fermentation.

We know today through the writings of Drs. Orian Truss and William Crook, authorities on fungus-related illnesses, that these foods contribute to an internal condition called polysystemic chronic candidiasis—a disorder that is said to affect one out of three Americans. This condition, which comes about through extended use of antibiotics, cortisone, and birth control pills, is fed by yeast-related foods and a high-carbohydrate diet. *The fungus that contributes to disease states is called* Candida albicans *and may be the basis of allergies, depression, and various environmental sensitivities.*

Despite my concern about the dietary imbalances I began to observe, my days at the Pritikin Center were personally fulfilling when I considered the overall successes. Our work made a difference in people's lives who were now much more aware of the need to eat sensibly and exercise regularly. All the while, I kept abreast of the latest health and nutritional research from doctors, clinics, and journals from around the world. As a health researcher, I continually sought nutritional answers to new illnesses and disorders such as food and chemical reactions, premenstrual syndrome, and *Candida albicans*. These new disorders began to surface and became as problematic as the degenerative diseases (such as heart disease) that the Pritikin diet was created to alleviate. There appeared to be a whole new generation of twenty-first-century health invaders that the Pritikin diet wasn't designed to address.

New Findings: It's in the Fat

I left Pritikin in 1982 to research the underlying causes of the newly discovered health invaders and incorporate the latest findings into the basic Pritikin prescription of diet and exercise. In search of more answers, I traveled to Europe to study the health techniques of different clinics. While the results in these clinics were impressive, the need for a practical way to enhance immunity and ward off disease was ignored.

Back in the United States, the most exciting research that surfaced identified certain kinds of fats with helping to control disease conditions:

- Fat from the Omega-3 fatty acid family found in fish oil was being used to treat heart disease, arthritis, migraines, and even cancer.

- GLA, an Omega-6 fatty acid found in certain botanical oils such as borage and evening primrose, was having great success in treat-

ing premenstrual syndrome, infertility, alcoholism, and immunity disorders.

While in the Pritikin view fat was the dietary cause of
most degenerative disease, the latest medical opinion
was that the *right* kind of fat was a panacea for most
diseases.

Pritikin said fat was the problem. I was seeing fat as
the solution.

I became more engrossed in the fat issue and found
that *fat is one of the most basic yet least understood
nutrients.* Pritikin was not wrong about the dangers of
polyunsaturated fats when he wrote: "In several respects
unsaturated fats may be worse for you than saturated
fats." But he didn't differentiate between the refined
and unrefined varieties. Leading health organizations
such as the American Heart Association suggest that
saturates should be replaced with polyunsaturates, but
they don't differentiate between the good and bad fats
either. The matter of refining fat is crucial. Refinement
destroys the essential fatty acids, which become unusable and harmful to the human body.

As a professional food educator, I was concerned
about how an indispensable food nutrient like fat could
become so dispensable. During the course of my research, I found out that the real problem was not so
much what fat was doing to us, but what we were doing
to fat.

Primary Factors That Devitalize and Alter Fats

- heat
- hydrogenation
- oxidation
- homogenization

The fate of all fat is determined basically by these
conditions. *These four factors can chemically change
the most widely consumed fatty food sources into foods*

unsuitable for human consumption. Commercial vegetable oil, margarine, and whole milk are prime examples of devitalized, even harmful foods because the fat content has been altered. The New Nutrition Diet will show you how fat has become misrepresented and misunderstood because of the health-destroying effects of heat, oxidation, hydrogenation, and homogenization.

Eat Fat and Lose Weight

You will learn, as I did, that not all fats are bad. As a matter of fact, the right kind and the right amount of fat is essential for good health and lasting weight loss.

Weight loss, you say? That's right. Weight loss is a completely unexpected benefit of eating the right kind of fat. My female patients who started supplementing their diets with foods or food supplements high in certain kinds of fat began to report surprising weight loss results. These women were not dieting, per se, but were prescribed a special fat nutrient, GLA, to control their PMS problems, recurring yeast infections, and arthritis. One woman who had a weight problem called me to say that not only was she elated over her cramp-free menstrual period but that she had somehow lost weight, too. She exclaimed, "I can't get over the fact that I'm eating fat and losing weight!"

The difference, of course, was the *right* kind of fat. The standing joke among my patients was how Pritikin's former Director of Nutrition was now promoting fat—what I told them was called an essential fat. Truth is stranger than fiction, I guess, because that was exactly what was happening. Fat was the answer to many menstrual problems suffered by my clients. Furthermore, fat was in to stay thin.

The weight loss phenomenon of the New Nutrition Diet became so popular in my private practice that I was getting referrals from clients who were encouraging their obese friends to see me. I had to find out what was really going on inside the body when the outside results were so dramatic.

I learned that *the right kind of fat—an essential fat— stimulates a mechanism in the body that in turn burns fat.* This internal fat burner is what scientists call "*brown fat.*" Brown fat may well be the most important discovery to explain why some people can remain thin while eating everything in sight while others, no matter how restricted their caloric intake, still cannot lose weight.

The Fat to Keep You Thin

There are basically two kinds of fat cells in the body: white fat and brown fat.

> • *White fat is the insulating fat layer under the skin that stores excess calories as fat.*

> • *Brown fat is a special fat-burning tissue that burns excess calories for heat rather than body energy.*

Most of what we know about brown fat has come from animal studies. Animals depend on their brown fat to keep them warm during hibernation. Brown fat alone generates one-fourth of the heat produced by all of the other body tissues combined. It apparently is a specially conditioned body warmer that operates when extra heat is needed.

Brown fat is located deeper in the body than white fat—in the thoracic area along the backbone and the back of the neck, and in the adrenal glands, kidneys, and aorta. The brown color is caused by the presence of concentrated fat-burning cellular units called mitochondria. The quest has been to find out what activates the mitochondria in the brown fat. What researchers discovered was that *thin people have "activated" brown fat, while overweight individuals have dormant brown fat.*

Also, brown fat decreases with age, which may account for why many people gain weight as they grow older. Whatever the age, brown fat needs the right kind of "activator" so the body will burn, rather than store, more calories. A breakthrough came when it was discovered that GLA—gamma linolenic acid—a special fat nutrient, was shown to "activate" brown fat. Clearly, because of its beneficial effects, GLA is an essential fat.

Studies now show that the addition of certain fats— essential fats—to the diet assists weight control, cardiovascular disorders, and a host of hair, skin, and nail conditions. Essential-fat deficiencies are linked to a weakened immune system that offers a defenseless home for viral, parasitic, and bacterial invaders that lead to modernday health problems.

The Solution

You can see why the key to my diet is none other than fat. Without it, more food is needed to satisfy your appetite and meet energy needs. Fat in the diet gives a sense of fullness, or satiety. When the body is fat-starved, one is hungry all the time, tending to overeat and binge particularly on carbohydrates (cookies, cakes, rolls, bagels, muffins). Excessive eating of grain carbohydrates (found in bread, cereal, and pasta, for example) can irritate the intestines if their intake is much greater than other foods because of sensitivity to gluten. The popularity of high-carbohydrate diets has magnified gluten sensitivity.

With small amounts of the correct fats, appetite will normalize, your weight will stabilize, and you will burn calories more efficiently. The natural result of all these efforts is lasting weight loss.

In a similar vein, this book will explain how the role of cholesterol in the diet and in the bloodstream has been unduly maligned. An elevated serum cholesterol level is a signal of improper fat metabolism caused primarily by too much processed fat. Our bodies need cholesterol for hormones, nerve impulse transmission, arterial lining, and bile salts for fat digestion. Did you know that over 80 percent of the brain's solid matter is made up of cholesterol? Just as not all fat is bad, neither is cholesterol all bad. Cholesterol is such a vital substance to the body that if sufficient amounts are not ingested from the diet, the body's own tissue (primarily the liver) will produce more to compensate for dietary lack. If there is too much absorbed from the diet, then the body will make less.

The unique Fat Flush program (see chapter 15, "The Two-Week Fat Flush") will remove accumulated and unecessary fats and unhealthy cholesterol buildup from your system. This two-week program highlights three major points:

Essential fat (in the form of safflower oil and dietary GLA supplements)
Fiber (contained in raw vegetables)
Fluid (10 glasses of water daily) This will prepare your body for the long-term MASTER MENU PLAN.

Each of these components has unique fat-fighting properties. For example, Long Life Cocktail, (see p. 151) with its cranberry juice base that acts as a carrier for powdered psyllium husks, is a powerful solvent that simultaneously dissolves unwanted fatty globules in the bloodstream and tissues and delivers beneficial fiber.

THE MASTER MENU PLAN goes beyond the *art* of cooking and explains the *science* of cooking. The 21-day sample menu plan (see "The New Nutrition Master Menu Plan," p. 159) is just that—a sample plan to give you an idea of how to put together a safe and healthy diet. The MASTER FORMULA preceding the plan can be used as a reference for your own menu planning and food selection. For this purpose, as well as to assist professionals in therapeutic diet planning, I have included an exchange list at the end of the recipe section ("Food Equivalents," p. 202). In addition to providing a 21-day sample menu plan and recipes, there is emphasis on the purchase, preparation, and storage of foods. These areas have a major impact on the quality of essential fat. Proper purchase, preparation, and storage will ensure the essential fat value of your diet and weight loss maintenance.

And what about exercise? The exercise plan represents another progression beyond most other exercise programs in that the New Nutrition Exercise Plan (chapter 11) is based first and foremost around sunlight. The aerobic exercise of choice is brisk walking. It is most desirable to do your walking outdoors in daylight, if possible, for at least 30 minutes a day. As long as it is done outdoors for a vigorous half-hour at least three times a week, you are following the basic exercise requirement. The outdoors is important here because of the added benefit of the full-spectrum light of the sun directly reaching the retina of the eye. When sun strikes the retina, a valuable electrical impulse is carried through the optic nerve to the mental, emotional, and physical centers of the brain. The physical center directly stimulates the temperature-regulating hypothalamus gland, which in turn stimulates the pituitary and pineal glands, which control all other endocrine functions. So, do not wear sunglasses. On the New Nutrition Diet, natural sunlight is an important nutrient.

Several years ago a Pritikin participant sent this poem to me in the mail:

> *Lord, grant me the strength that I may not fall*
> *Into the clutches of cholesterol.*
> *At polyunsaturates I'll never mutter,*
> *For the road to hell is paved with butter.*
> *And cake is cursed and cream is awful*
> *And Satan is hiding in every waffle.*
> *Beelzebub is a chocolate drop*
> *And Lucifer is a lollypop*
> *Teach me the evils of hollandaise*
> *Of pasta and gobs of mayonnaise,*

And crisp fried chicken from the South—
Lord, if you love me, shut my mouth!
                                (Author unknown)

The New Nutrition Diet philosophy, unlike the stringent Pritikin principles, is not about denial. Rather, the New Nutrition Diet is a lifelong plan tailored to the lifestyles and nutritional needs of America today. Fat is not to be feared; instead, it's to be better understood. The New Nutrition Diet has adapted the basic Pritikin concepts to the latest research on the essential dietary role of fat for better health. The Pritikin principles that have revolutionized our eating habits in the past decades have now been expanded to ensure a healthy future of easier weight loss, continuous weight maintenance, and a fortified immune system.

3

ALL ABOUT
ESSENTIAL FATS

Life is largely a matter of chemistry.
—WILLIAM J. MAYO, M.D.

In order to identify the essential fats among all other fats, we need to understand more about fats in general and answer two important questions:

1. How have fats been optimally designed to work in the body?
2. How can fats become destructive rather than constructive dietetic elements when damaged by food processing and cooking?

Damaged fats are unnatural substances that are biochemically inactive and cannot be utilized by the body. They interfere with the metabolism of natural fats and thereby impede every function of the human body, right down to the cellular level. They weaken cell membranes, suppress the immune system, and block the prostaglandins that act as the "master switch" that regulates and controls almost all cellular activity second-by-second.

Ironically, the smallest changes in the molecular structure of natural fats can have devastating effects on body chemistry. As you will learn, as I did, this can mean the difference between effortless weight loss or weight gain, regeneration or degeneration, health or disease. These differences, and what distinguishes good fat from bad, are what essential fat is all about.

The most direct way to learn about essential fat is to

start with some fundamental concepts and simple biochemistry. So, let us begin with the basic definition that all fats, essential fats included, are known as *lipids*. Lipids include fats, oils, and fatlike substances that are greasy, such as cholesterol, butterfat, and vegetable oil, for example. Lipids are not water soluble, but are soluble in alcohol, detergents, and organic solvents like gasoline.

When we speak of fats, we refer to both fats and oils. The difference between them is that fats are solid at room temperature, whereas oils are liquid. Dietary fat is available primarily from two basic sources: animal and vegetable. Animal fats tend to be solid and vegetable fats tend to be liquid.

Fats, proteins, and carbohydrates are the three fundamental building blocks for creating and maintaining life. Each of these three nutrient groups contains the basic chemical elements of life itself: hydrogen, carbon, and oxygen. Compared with protein and carbohydrates, fats contain less oxygen and more available carbon and hydrogen. Since carbon and hydrogen can be burned for energy, fats are our most concentrated energy source and have more calories per gram. Fats contain 9 calories per gram, as compared with 4 calories per gram from proteins and carbohydrates. A little fat goes a long way.

Basic Fat Groups

There are three primary fatty acid types: saturates, monounsaturates, and polyunsaturates. All foods contain a mixture of all types of fatty acids, but one usually predominates. The predominant fatty acid determines how fats are classified.

Here are the fats:

Saturates	Animal sources: pork, lamb, and beef fats (lard, tallow, suet), or-

gan meats, full-fat dairy products such as whole milk, cream cheese, ice cream, and butter. Vegetable sources: coconut oil, cocoa butter, palm oil, and palm-kernel oil, found in commercially prepared baked goods, pie fillings, nondairy cream substitutes, and fast-food preparation.

Monounsaturates

Vegetable, legume, and seed sources: olive oil, avocado, peanut, and canola oil. (Canola oil is made from rapeseed oil, the most popular cooking oil in eastern Europe, China, India, and Canada.)

Polyunsaturates (Omega-3)

Animal sources: mother's milk, marine oils from salmon, mackerel, herring, cod, sardines, rainbow trout, shrimp, oysters, halibut, tuna, sablefish, bass, flounder, and anchovies; cold-water fish such as trout and crappie.
Vegetable sources: linseed oil, flaxseed, soybeans, walnuts, wheat germ, wheat sprouts, fresh sea vegetation, leafy greens.

Polyunsaturates (Omega-6)

Animal sources: mother's milk, organ meats, lean meats.
Vegetable sources: safflower, sunflower, corn, soy, cottonseed, sesame, raw nuts and seeds, legumes, spirulina, leafy greens.
Botanicals: borage, evening primrose, and gooseberry oils.

How Fats Work in the Body

At their biochemical best and in nature's form, fats serve many invaluable functions. They are the most potent energy source available to the body. Gram for gram, fat yields more than twice as much energy as either carbohydrate or protein. *As storage for the body's excess calories, all excess carbohydrate and protein calories are also stored as body fat.*

Fats are the major constituent of all cell membranes in the body. By maintaining strong cell membranes, they help protect against invading allergens, bacteria, and viruses. The cell membranes are the body's defense system. Increased permeability can have devastating effects on any body tissue, allowing toxins a passageway into the bloodstream.

In babies, fat is needed in the formation of myelin—a specialized membrane that protects the nerves and is essential to the normal development of the central nervous system and the brain. This development is best met by the fat contained in breast milk. Second best is the fat derived from vegetable oil added in formula preparation. The use of skim milk in the diet of a child younger than age 2 is not recommended because of the need for essential fatty acids. At all other ages human beings must get essential fats through certain unprocessed vegetable oils or fish sources.

Perhaps the most important role of fats is in the manufacture of prostaglandins (see chapter 5, "The New Nutrition Diet Prostaglandin Protection"), hormonelike compounds that regulate every function in the human body at the molecular level. Because the system does not store prostaglandins, each cell needs a daily amount of essential fat to produce them.

Besides the powerful prostaglandin production, there are other life-supporting functions of fat. These include:

- Assisting the body in utilizing the B vitamins for digestion, nerve health, energy, and mental well-being
- Elevating calcium levels in the bloodstream and transporting it to the tissues for strong bones and cramp-free muscles that are toned and firm
- Carrying and storing fat-soluble vitamins such as A, D, E, and K for healthy skin, reproduction, and blood clotting
- Activating the flow of bile (a fat digestant in the gall bladder)
- Helping the body conserve protein to rebuild vital tissues
- Assisting in maintaining normal temperature
- Insulating and cushioning the vital organs, nerves, and muscles against shock, heat, and cold
- Sealing in moisture for healthier skin, hair, and nails

In terms of cooking, fat is an irreplaceable assistant. Salad dressings, stir sautés, and marinades taste flat without the rich flavor that fat imparts. Fat is one of the most vital ingredients in a health-conscious kitchen because it seals in delicate food flavors, keeps food hot, and contributes to juiciness, color, and texture.

Happily for all of us, a diet with healthy fats leaves you satisfied. Fat delays hunger by depressing gastric secretion and slowing down the emptying time for the stomach. Because fats are more slowly digested, they leave you satisfied longer.

The Infamous Four

The question is: Why aren't all fats considered healthy fats? The answer can be found in the commercial oil-processing plant and in the privacy of your kitchen.

A fat can be damaged by four invisible factors that I
call the Infamous Four: (1) heat, (2) hydrogenation, (3)
oxygen, and (4) homogenization. Unfortunately, we often cannot see, taste, or smell the damage caused by
these factors, yet all of them create unnatural changes
in fatty acid structure. It is important to recognize these
four factors so you can protect your foods from them by
proper selection, preparation, cooking, and storage practices. Avoiding damaged fats will assist you in optimiz-
ing weight loss, beauty, and immunity, as well as
protecting you from degenerative disease.

The Heat Factor

Oils are commercially processed to improve shelf life,
flavor, smell, and color. They are purified to remove the
fat-soluble agricultural residues so prevalent in major
food crops such as soybeans, wheat, and corn. Unfortunately, due to the high temperatures involved (sometimes up to 475 degrees), polyunsaturated fatty acids
are converted from the naturally occurring, beneficial
"cis" form to the unnatural, harmful "trans" form. Cis
fats melt at 55 degrees, below the body temperature of
98.6, which makes them fully available to the system.
Trans fats, on the other hand, melt at up to 111 degrees,
so they remain solid, and therefore unmetabolized, in
the human body.

The Hydrogenation Factor

The hydrogenation process that converts liquid oils into
hardened fats, such as margarine and vegetable shortening, destroys natural fatty acids in even greater numbers by converting the natural fatty acid form into the
biologically impaired trans form. While hydrogenated
oil may be more stable than unhydrogenated oil, the
trans-fat factor strips the essential fatty acids of their

biological potency. Trans-fatty acids cannot be used by the body to produce prostaglandins and furthermore impair the normal use of cis-fatty acids. Trans-fatty acids are rarely found in nature but are predominant in commercial salad oil (15 percent) and hydrogenated products such as margarine (30 percent) and shortening (47 percent).

The Oxygen Factor

Oils are more susceptible to oxygen once they have been extracted from their source. Interaction with oxygen creates peroxides, or free radicals, that cause rancidity. Oxygen then becomes less available for its major bodily roles of respiration and detoxification.

Unsaturates are more sensitive to oxygen than saturates due to their biochemical composition of double bonds. "Poly"unsaturates contain multiple double bonds and therefore have more potential sites to which oxygen can attach. They are more likely to become oxidized or rancid than either the saturates or monounsaturates. In other words, the more unsaturated an oil is, the quicker it can become rancid.

The oxidation of oils also is related to temperature. Refrigerated oils do not become rancid as quickly as when they are left out at room temperature. Heated oils oxidize very rapidly. At frying temperatures (above 300 degrees), polyunsaturated oils not only rapidly oxidize but are converted from the cis form to the "trans" form. The commercial practice of reusing frying oils raises the specter of both trans and oxidized fats to the most dangerous levels.

Exposure to air when using or storing oil is another way for oxygen to enter the scene. Natural oils contain substances called antioxidants that protect the oil from rancidity; however, these substances, like lecithin and vitamin E, are removed or destroyed during the refining process.

Polyunsaturates can also oxidize inside the body. They can react with normal byproducts of cellular metabolism as well as environmental pollutants such as smog, X-rays, cigarette smoke, chemicals, exhaust, and trace metals such as copper, nickel, and iron.

Technically, when polyunsaturates oxidize, they produce "free radicals," a term that has become synonymous with cell and tissue destruction. Free radicals are actually highly reactive molecular fragments that are in search of stability. They need electrons for their stability, and they try to pick them up from other molecules, creating a chain reaction that damages the cells. Normal cells take on a burnt appearance. Premature aging, heart disease, cancer, and other degenerative processes are the result of unbridled free radical activity.

This free radical degeneration will continue unless the free radicals are neutralized by antioxidant substances that pair up their electrons. These substances are vitamins E and C, beta carotene, selenium, and the body's own enzymes.

The Homogenization Factor

Homogenization, a process that extends shelf life, is another common technique that damages fats. Normal milk fat occurs in large globules that are usually digested intact in the intestinal tract. Homogenization breaks up these fat globules into extremely small droplets (one-third the original size) that are dispersed into the milk.

According to leading cardiac specialist and researcher, Dr. Kurt A. Oster, Chief of Cardiology Emeritus at Park City Hospital, Bridgeport, Connecticut, much of the homogenized fat particles can bypass digestion and absorb directly into the bloodstream, carrying with them a destructive enzyme called xanthine oxidase (XO), that is protected by liposomes (membranelike packets). As it is carried through the bloodstream, XO can damage the arteries by attacking plasmalogen, an integral part of the artery wall and heart tissue. This results in a lesion on the artery wall. The weakened tissue then attracts cholesterol and fat, which coat the arterial lesion, soothing and smoothing the injury to promote healing. When this happens, plaque buildup results and coronary disease occurs because of constriction created by the concentration of cholesterol. Cholesterol can be compared to the Good Samaritan at the scene of the crime.

The primary opposition to Dr. Oster's XO theory comes from researchers who argue that the XO molecule is simply too large to be absorbed into the bloodstream without first being destroyed by the digestive process. Dr. Oster counters with the fact that the fatal food-poisoning bacteria that causes botulism is even larger than XO and yet is somehow absorbed into the bloodstream without first being destroyed in the digestive tract.

Besides xanthine oxidase, there are other reasons for avoiding milk. Milk may be a contributing cause of arthritis, allergy, and asthma. It may be helpful to eliminate all dairy products for at least three weeks if you have any of these problems. If your condition improves, then look for milk substitutes for a longer time.

Many people are concerned about osteoporosis and so drink milk for its high calcium content. It is interesting to note, however, that those countries that have the highest consumption of dairy products—the United States, Finland, Britain, Sweden, and Israel—also evidence the highest rates of osteoporosis. There are other minerals besides calcium that may be just as important in the prevention and management of osteoporosis. Manganese is one of them.

Dr. Paul Saltman, at the University of California at San Diego, evaluated blood and bone samples of women with severe osteoporosis and women with no sign of osteoporosis. The only striking difference was the blood levels of manganese in the two groups. The osteoporotic women had a manganese level one-quarter of the level of the other group. Manganese deficiency has also been linked with diabetes because of its connection with insulin release. Besides blood sugar, manganese deficiency is connected to disk problems and cartilage formation. Manganese can be found in red meat, nuts, seeds, eggs, and salad greens.

On the New Nutrition Diet only nonfat milk (skim milk) that reads 0 fat grams on the label is recommended. Without any fat, there is no XO that can be carried into the body's tissues. Low-fat milk (the 2 percent variety), with a 5-gram fat content per cup, actually derives 36 percent of its calories from fat and thus contains a sufficient fat content to be a potent XO carrier. If you insist on continuing to drink 2 percent milk, boil it before drinking. Heat deactivates XO.

4

THE NEW NUTRITION DIET WEIGHT LOSS CONNECTION

*The popularity of dieting proves
that people will go to great lengths to
avoid going to great widths.*
—CARL OTTAVI
newspaper columnist and humorist

Obesity, a major national health problem, may be easily overcome with essential fats without the health risks associated with dieting. Despite the myriad diets and the abundance of fitness information, America has been growing even fatter. Look at the facts:

- Ninety percent of all Americans think they are overweight.
- Ninety-seven percent of people who go on a diet regain all the weight or more within two years.
- Approximately 15 percent of children and 20 percent of teens are overweight.
- About 25 percent of men and women between the ages of 20 and 74 are clinically obese (i.e., 20 percent above normal weight).
- Over 35 percent of dieters have a goal of losing 15 pounds or more.

With statistics like these, it is little wonder that the United States has a national obsession with dieting.

Unfortunately, going on a fad diet usually creates what is referred to as the yo-yo syndrome, whereby the dieter later regains more weight than was originally lost. The cycle of sizable weight loss/gain results in higher and higher weight regain. During the weight loss phase of crash diets, both muscle tissue and fat are lost. During the rebound phase, the weight regained is pure fat. This results in an increase in the size of fat cells and a greater capacity for storing fat.

When calories are abruptly restricted, there is another negative consequence: the body slows down its metabolic rate to allow it to function on less energy, and therefore fewer calories are burned. This process was evolved in our ancestors to allow them to survive the long famines that were common in those times.

There is recent evidence that every time a dieter loses and regains weight, plaque is deposited in the arteries, which leads to atherosclerosis, a prime underlying cause of heart disease. On severely restricted diets, heart muscle tissue can also be lost, causing irregular heartbeat and other more serious dysfunctions. While quick-weight-loss fad diets have proliferated, the statistics show we are not winning the war on fat.

The problem in America is one of excess. Obesity is rated our Number One health hazard that underlies most of our degenerative diseases. In 1984 the Department of Health and Human Sciences released some statistics about the major causes of death in America. The numbers are as follows:

Causes of Death in the United States

Stroke	76.6%
Heart disease	37.4%
Cancer	22.1%
Accidents	4.5%
Lung disease	3.4%
Pneumonia, influenza	2.9%
Diabetes	1.8%
Suicide	1.4%

Most of these leading causes of death are weight related. The obese are at greater risk to heart and circulatory diseases, cancer, respiratory problems, diabetes, and accidents. Other risks include greater surgical complications and pregnancy difficulties. The more overweight, the greater the risk. Excess fat strains every organ in the body.

For many people, it is extremely difficult to lose weight. When calories are restricted, our metabolic rates can adjust downward, matching the lack of food. As previously mentioned, we inherited this response from our ancestors, who needed to be able to survive seasonal fluctuations in food availability. This mechanism is especially active in women because of the added energy demands of bearing children. Because of this, simply restricting calories is often ineffective for lasting weight loss.

Effective weight loss requires affecting your metabolic rate. In my practice, I found that many women were effortlessly losing weight when taking supplements of an essential fatty acid for premenstrual symptoms such as fluid retention, cramps, and irritability. In some way, this essential fatty acid was stimulating their metabolic rates. In the scientific literature there is a study that shows that evening primrose oil enabled individuals at least 10 percent over their ideal weight to lose weight without dieting. Those individuals who were within 10 percent of their ideal weight did not lose weight, indicating that their metabolisms were already at normal efficiency. The key fat nutrient in the evening primrose oil was GLA. It was activating their brown-fat metabolism.

Brown Fat

As you now know, brown fat is a high-energy type of fat whose sole function is to burn calories for heat rather than depositing them for storage. It is your personal *fat burner*. Although brown fat comprises only 10 percent or less of total body fat, it burns one-fourth of all the calories burned by the other fat tissues combined. Brown fat is brown because it contains numerous mitochondria, little fat-burning factories. The rest of the fat in the body is white because it contains few mitochondria. White fat is the insulating layer on the outside of the body, just under the skin. Brown fat lies deeper, surrounding the organs such as the heart, kidneys, and adrenals, as well as the neck, spine, and major thoracic blood vessels. While everybody has a fat burner, they are not all equally active. The thin person who has an actively functioning fat burner can easily convert excess calories into body heat. The obese person, eating the same number of calories, will store them as white fat instead.

In the case of two of my clients, both professional models, it was not until particular salad dressings were added to their diets that those last stubborn 5 pounds were metabolized and lost. For years these women followed the nutritionally chic high-carbohydrate regimens. They ate lots of vegetables, whole-grain cereals, and potatoes without butter. While this routine worked for them in the beginning, after a while their weight reached a plateau and the scale would not budge. They came to me with complaints of dry hair, skin, and nails, and the need to lose more weight for upcoming photo sessions. Within one week of following the New Nutrition Diet, the scale finally moved downward. The only dietary change was the addition of two tablespoons of unprocessed safflower oil in the form of salad dressing. Within three weeks, their hair, skin, and nails were noticeably improved. Something remarkable was happening.

The GLA and the safflower oil that helped weight loss are clearly related to each other. Safflower oil is one of the richest sources of the essential fatty acid cis-linoleic acid. In normal metabolism within the body, cis-linoleic acid is converted into GLA. In many ways, however, this conversion is impaired. If cis-linoleic acid is heated, for example, some of it is converted into trans-linoleic acid, an unnatural fatty acid that not only cannot be converted into GLA but inhibits the conversion of the rest of the cis-linoleic acid into GLA. Safflower oil is frequently heated during commercial manufacturing and in home cooking. Even higher levels of trans-linoleic acid are produced when vegetable oils are hydrogenated into margarines.

Other factors that interfere with GLA synthesis are excessive saturated fats, alcohol, cigarette smoking, caffeine, cholesterol, old age, and deficiencies in zinc, magnesium, and vitamin B-6. These factors are quite common and make the production of GLA from linoleic acid unreliable. This is why preformed GLA is preferred.

As a nutritionist, I was taught that we receive plenty of the essential fatty acids—namely, cis-linoleic acid—from dietary vegetable oils like safflower, sunflower, and corn oils. But, as I learned, when oils are processed to extend shelf life or to become margarine, the cis-linoleic acid becomes trans-linoleic acid, a malfunctioning fat. Trans fats are contained in almost all forms of baked products such as breads, cookies, and cakes, where hydrogenated vegetable oil or vegetable shortening appear on the list of ingredients. Without full biological vitality, the refined and altered oils deprive the body of its weight loss capability.

Although the typical American diet is lower in fat calories, at 40 percent, than the original Eskimo diet, at 70 percent, most of our fat comes from damaged fat sources such as commercial vegetable oils (heat damaged), french fries and potato chips (heat damaged and oxidized), margarine and baked goods (hydrogenated), and dairy products (homogenized). None of these food sources is capable of providing fat-burning GLA. These damaged fat sources render fat biologically impotent.

The Big Picture

Fats are everywhere. It is easy to recognize visible fats in foods, but sometimes the fats cannot be identified by

sight. While obvious visible fats such as butter, processed vegetable oil, and salad dressing are easier to
control, the hidden fats in the creamy cheese sauces,
heavily marbled meats, and flaky pie crusts are more
challenging to identify. Avoiding the damaged fat that
accompanies invisible fat can also be difficult. The best
way, of course, to protect yourself from bad fats is to
avoid all foods in which the fat source has been heated,
hydrogenated, oxidized, or homogenized.

Finding your way through the fat maze therefore takes
planning and know-how. To really see more clearly
what you're up against, here is a chart that classifies
food according to the percentage of calories from fat.
Look at the chart to see how much fat is hidden in
everyday foods. At this point you need not be overly
concerned about being able to identify how much of
the hidden fat is also damaged fat. Chapter 16, ''The
New Nutrition Diet Prescription,'' offers specific guidelines that will keep you on a healthy and essential fat
course.

Percentages of Fat Calories Found in Foods

More than 90%	Whipped cream, pork sausage, cooking oils, margarine, butter, gravy, mayonnaise
More than 80%	Spare ribs, bologna, cream cheese, salad dressing
More than 70%	Half and half, peanuts, hot dogs, pork chops, cheddar cheese, sirloin steak, bacon, lamb chops, pecans, macadamia nuts
More than 60%	Potato chips, regular ground beef, ham, eggs
More than 50%	Round steak, pot roast, creamed soups, ice cream, sweet rolls

More than 40%	Whole milk, cake, doughnuts, french fries
More than 30%	Muffins, chicken, cookies, fruit pie, creamed cottage cheese, tuna fish, low-fat milk
More than 20%	Crackers, ice milk, crab meat, beef liver, lean fish
More than 10%	Bread, pretzels
Less than 10%	Sherbet, nonfat milk, most fruits and vegetables, egg whites, baked potato

(Adapted from the Public Health Nutrition Service, Rhode Island Department of Health.)

5

THE NEW NUTRITION DIET PROSTAGLANDIN PROTECTION

A salmon a day keeps a coronary away.
—Medical World News

In addition to weight control, the power of essential fats is found in their conversion into prostaglandins. Prostaglandins are short-lived hormonelike substances that regulate metabolic processes throughout the body at the cellular level. They were discovered over fifty years ago in the prostate gland, hence the name prostaglandins. Then, in the 1960s, it was discovered that they were to be found in almost every cell of the body.

The discovery of prostaglandins may be the greatest nutritional finding of the century because of their far-reaching implications. They have been found to control a wide range of activities including immune response, inflammation, reproduction, blood clotting, blood pressure, tumor growth, brain function, and allergies. New properties of prostaglandins are being reported continually. So important and monumental is the prostaglandin connection to health that the 1982 Nobel Prize in medicine was awarded to scientists in prostaglandin research.

Prostaglandins can only be made from two fatty acids: GLA, the Omega-6 fatty acid, and EPA, the Omega-3 fatty acid. While there are eight essential fatty acids in total, only these two are the direct prostaglandin building blocks. The prostaglandins formed by GLA and EPA have different functions. Together, the two nutrients form an unbeatable health combination.

Unrefined vegetable oils contain the GLA raw material, cis-linoleic acid, which the body converts to useful GLA. GLA, in turn, produces prostaglandin E1 (known as PGE1) and, to a lesser degree, PGE2 (see The Prostaglandin Factor diagram, p. 43). GLA is directly contained in a few major sources, such as mother's milk, borage, seeds of the evening primrose, gooseberry, and spirulina, a type of plankton. While black currant contains 17 percent GLA, making it a high GLA source, it also contains a high amount of another fatty acid called alpha-linolenic acid (ALA), which inhibits the metabolism of GLA into prostaglandins. Other sources of ALA, such as linseed and soybean oils, are not recommended for GLA supplementation because they will also impede GLA development.

The direct form of EPA is found in high amounts in cold-water-fish oils from fatty fish such as sardines, salmon, and mackerel. It then converts into PGE3.

Neither the unprocessed vegetable oils nor the Omega-3 fish oils can be converted into prostaglandins without the presence of specific catalysts. Known as enzymatic cofactors, these catalysts are vitamins B-3 (niacin), B-6, and C, and the minerals magnesium and zinc. Unfortunately, in the typical American diet, deficiencies of these nutrients are quite common because of soil depletion, food processing, and poor eating practices.

The presence of the trans-fatty acids from commercially processed oils, hydrogenated margarines, and fried foods interferes with the transformation of GLA and EPA into prostaglandins. *Without the ability to transform into prostaglandins, the essential fatty acids are biologically worthless.*

There are several other factors that hamper prostaglandin production by blocking the enzyme that transforms cis-linoleic acid into GLA. These factors include saturated fats, cholesterol, aging, alcohol, high blood sugar (diabetes), viral infection, radiation, and aspirin. The following diagram gives a detailed illustration of what substances act as blocking factors to the effective metabolism of prostaglandins from essential fatty acids.

The Prostaglandin Factor

Metabolic conversion of essential fatty acids to prostaglandins and common blocking factors of GLA and EPA production:

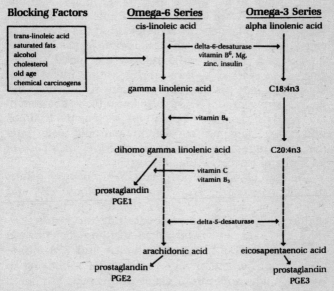

Vitamin Research Products Notes, April 1986, vol. 1, no. 2, 2044 Old Middlefield Way, Mountain View, CA 94043. (800) 541-1623

The Benefits of Prostaglandins

Reports about new uses of essential fats appear almost daily around the world regarding health benefits of prostaglandins. Prostaglandins have single-handedly turned around medicine's negative regard for fat into an extraordinary appreciation of its true biological function. Essential fats may be the savior of twentieth-century disease conditions and immune disorders.

The benefits of essential fats are far-reaching. Cardiovascular disease—America's Number One Killer—has been shown to be related to good fat intake. Fish oils containing EPA are known, for example, to reduce the stickiness of platelets, thereby lowering the chances of unwanted blood clots, the immediate cause of heart attacks and strokes. PGE3 relaxes the blood vessels, preventing arterial spasms and lowering blood pressure. This may also be the mechanism by which migraines are relieved. Fish oils also lower blood cholesterol and triglyceride levels. Populations such as the Eskimos and coastal Japanese consistently eat cold water fatty fish and subsequently have a much lower incidence of all forms of cardiovascular disease.

The high blood sugar associated with diabetes results in high triglyceride (fat) levels in the blood. EPA and PGE3 lower triglyceride levels, thereby decreasing the incidence of vascular disease affecting the hearts, kidneys, and eyes of diabetics. Since insulin deficiency is a common blocking factor of both GLA and EPA formation, supplementation may prove to be a blessing to diabetics who suffer from deficient prostaglandin functioning characterized by nerve twitching, infection, and sexual dysfunction.

Researchers are now studying the Omega-3 fish oils in the prevention and treatment of cancer. The therapeutic activity of beneficial prostaglandins may protect against cancer by strengthening the immune system.

It is important to point out, however, that not all

prostaglandins are good. While some suppress inflammation, others actually stimulate it. The prostaglandin known as PGE2 causes inflammation and is produced from arachidonic acid (see diagram, p. 43), a common fatty acid found in peanuts, land animal meats, and dairy products. PGE1 and PGE3, on the other hand, found in unrefined vegetable oils, linseed oil, and marine fish oils, suppress inflammation. It is obvious that because the inflammatory prostaglandins are synthesized from different essential fatty acids contained in various foods, diet affects prostaglandin production and the level of inflammation. Excessive red meat, milk, and cheese consumption have the potential of creating the inflammatory type of prostaglandins. Since many diseases have inflammation as an underlying condition, it is important to restrict the intake of these foods.

Early essential fatty acid studies involving linoleic acid showed marginal improvements in cases of eczema, psoriasis, and acne. Recent work with GLA and EPA have shown much better results, especially in combination with zinc and vitamin A. Bottle-fed babies with eczema respond very rapidly to oral and topical application of GLA-containing oils. One multiple sclerosis patient with eczema showed great improvement on GLA. The eczema returned when GLA was discontinued, and again disappeared when GLA was resumed. My patients frequently report that they receive compliments on their complexions when they follow the New Nutrition Diet, which promotes essential-fat intake. Their nails are also strengthened and dandruff flaking disappears.

The good news continues. Arthritics experience less pain and joint stiffness when consuming fish oils. Both GLA and EPA seem to significantly slow the progression of multiple sclerosis, an inflammatory autoimmune disease of the central nervous system.

By incorporating into the structure of the cellular membrane, essential fats decrease the permeability of vital tissues and organs. In the case of systemic yeast infection, this is particularly helpful. Essential fats can prevent yeast from spreading into the bloodstream from its normal intestinal and/or vaginal environs. The yeast cannot pass through the intestinal walls into the circulatory system when the mucous membrane lining of the digestive tract is strengthened by essential fats.

Omega-3 and Omega-6 fatty acids are also centrally involved in numerous brain disorders including schizophrenia, depression, and hyperactivity. Essential fat supplementation can reduce alcohol withdrawal symptoms and lessen the severity of hangovers.

So many diseases are being linked to essential fat metabolism and the prostaglandins every day that this discussion will no doubt be incomplete by the time you read this book. As an example, it was recently found that dry eyes and mouth responded to GLA supplementation. The normalization of tear production is certainly good news for contact lens wearers whose eyes are chronically dry and irritated.

However, a challenge remains: to translate the new clinical findings from laboratories all over the world into practical dietary guidelines that the American public can understand and follow. The New Nutrition Diet is the first step in that direction.

6

POLYUNSATURATES: GOOD FATS GONE BAD

*Nutriment is not nutriment if it
have not its power ... Nutriment
in name, not in deed.*
— Hippocrates

Commercially processed vegetable oils have suffered the
same nutritionally deprived fate as processed whole-
grain products. A pamphlet entitled "The Oil Story"
from the Organic Merchants Association points this out
quite graphically:

> The process of refining oils is exactly analogous
> to the refining of whole wheat, and whole sugar,
> into white ones. In all cases, one takes a product
> full of natural vitamins, minerals, enzymes and other
> food factors, and reduces the original natural food
> into a relative non-food, devitalized and stripped.

Despite their poor nutritional status, the consumption of vegetable oils has increased dramatically in recent years. In 1960, Americans consumed an average of
forty-five pounds of oils per year per person. By 1980
the figure had jumped to sixty pounds. In 1978 there
were over three hundred brands of vegetable oil on the
market. This increase has been due largely to oil company advertising campaigns that hype the cholesterol-
free state of vegetable oils. Vegetable oils are naturally
cholesterol-free because cholesterol is found only in
animal foods, not vegetables.

Oils were not always as nutritionally deprived as they are today. In the early 1900s, vegetable oils were made by pressing seeds, beans, and vegetables with large rollers. This cold-pressed oil was a healthy, whole substance rich in nutrients from the original food sources, high in lecithin, magnesium, and vitamins E and B-6. This nutritious oil had several economic drawbacks, however. First, the pressing method left too much oil in the pulp. Next, the oil itself became rancid quickly and needed refrigeration for storage. Last, it was strongly flavored, dark in color, and cloudy with sediment. So, in the 1920s, more complex refining procedures were introduced involving heating practices and chemical solvents that increased oil yield, improved stability, lightened color, and removed odor. This made for increased consumer appeal and better marketability. The more highly refined oils did not become rancid and so gained a longer shelf life. They required no refrigeration and so could be transported all over the country without freshness problems. The tasteless, colorless, aroma-free oil was more attractive to consumers who equated uniformity in color, taste, and texture with product wholesomeness. Consumers made the same mistake in choosing white flour over whole-wheat flour.

The health drawbacks of these modern processing methods were subtle but far-reaching. They removed nutrients and added unhealthy trans fats and solvent residues to a once healthy food.

Because of the higher heat generated, the beneficial cis form of essential fatty acids was converted into the unnatural trans form. Remember, trans fats prevent linoleic acid from activating into the GLA so vital for weight loss and the prostaglandins that control every cell in the body.

Even oils inaccurately labeled "cold pressed" have been extracted by the expeller or mechanical method that exposes the oil to temperatures ranging from 140 to 160 degrees. Furthermore, high temperatures are also used to precook seeds and break down tough outer layers for better oil yield. The term *cold pressed* is misleading to some degree because heat is involved in the cooking and pressing process, but it does mean that the oils have not been exposed to chemical solvents.

Most of the vegetable oils found on supermarket shelves are extracted with chemical solvents such as hexane, a chemical relative to gasoline. Hexane has irritating effects on the central nervous system and the lungs.

Both the expeller-pressed and solvent-extracted oils must go through further stages of purification to make them safe for human consumption. They are degummed to remove free fatty acids, then bleached and deodorized to remove pesticides and herbicides containing lead and arsenic, which are fat-soluble.

To ensure the most suitable oil for dietary use, look for the words *expeller pressed* or *crude* on the label. Remember that "crude" *does* mean purified of environmental contaminants. These words signal that the basic oil at least has not been solvent-extracted.

Keep in mind that commercial mayonnaise is made from heat-damaged, processed oils, as are corn chips, potato chips, and liquid egg substitutes. Numerous other condiments, such as tartar sauce, horseradish sauce, salad dressing, mayonnaise substitutes, and low-calorie mayonnaise usually contain processed oils. Furthermore, partially hydrogenated or hardened vegetable oils can be found in all margarines and most cookies, crackers, pie crusts, taco shells, dips, dessert toppings, cocoa and coffee mixes that use water instead of milk, nondairy coffee creamers, candy bars, and some frozen vegetables with sauce and some other frozen food entrees.

What Are the Essential Fats?

Essential fats are polyunsaturates that are properly manufactured to retain whole-food values. They are unhydrogenated and stored without exposure to heat or oxygen. Because polyunsaturates are more susceptible to heat and oxygen due to the greater number of double bonds, they should be consumed raw and should not be used for cooking, and especially not for frying.

The daily amount of essential fatty acids recommended for optimum health for most people can be found in two tablespoons of essential fat. Because of greater nutritional needs, children and pregnant or breast-feeding women can increase the daily amount to three tablespoons.

Margarine: From Bad to Worse

Vegetable oils that are hydrogenated are made into margarine and shortening by the addition of hydrogen atoms (see the diagram below). While most vegetable oils are slightly hydrogenated, margarine can be partially or fully

**The Hydrogenation of Unsaturated
to Saturated Fats**

Unsaturated   Saturated

hydrogenated. The hydrogenation process gives the product a longer shelf life and raises its melting point. This allows liquid vegetable oils to be turned into solid margarine. Vegetable shortening, the most highly hydrogenated product, lasts forever. Its long shelf life is a phenomenon of unnaturally saturated trans fat.

Hydrogenated fats offer many cooking conveniences at the expense of health, as we soon shall see. Convenience factors resulting from the hydrogenation process include an extended shelf life and neutralization of strong odors, tastes, and flavors. Hydrogenated vegetable shortenings are great for baking, and because of their durability they are very economical for large-scale institutional cooking and baking.

Vegetable shortening was first developed in the early 1900s by the English, who used whale oil in their product. By 1911, hydrogenated cooking fat from cottonseed oil was being sold commercially in the United States by Procter & Gamble under the product name Crisco. The miraculous new process of hydrogenation spawned a whole new industry and way of life in the ensuing decades.

"Butterine," the early name for Oleo margarine, was introduced in the 1930s. At that time, Oleo was a white shortening. Early margarine sales were slow, however, probably because consumers didn't like the lardlike appearance of margarine.

The butter industry fought the coloring of margarine for many years. However, by 1952 colored margarine was legalized in every state except Wisconsin and Minnesota. Later, these two strong dairy states legalized the coloring of margarine and sales boomed.

Today, margarine outsells butter. In its heyday, margarine topped butter sales by 100 million pounds per year. The average American consumes ten pounds of shortening and twenty pounds of margarine per year.

Hydrogenation opened the door to fast food and its deep-fried offerings. Unfortunately, this has opened the door to a new variety of diseases. To begin with, the process of hydrogenation has converted the original naturally unsaturated fatty acids into unnaturally saturated fatty acids and trans fats to a staggering degree, up to 47 percent of some margarines. Trans fats block prostaglandin production. Remember, prostaglandins control vital functions such as blood-fat levels, blood pressure, platelet clumping, and formation of red blood cells.

Perhaps most dangerous of all, these trans fats create weakened cell membranes, which are more permeable to viruses and bacteria of all kinds, seriously compromising the body's defense system. To add insult to injury, trans fats are defective fats that cannot be activated into the prostaglandins, which have such far-reaching metabolic effects throughout the body. Research by Dr. Fred Kummerow confirmed the atherosclerotic effects of margarine on test animals in 1974.

Unhealthy additives such as benzoic acid or sodium benzoate are also added to margarine as antibacterial and antifungal agents. Most suspect of all is the use of nickel in the making of margarine and vegetable shortening. Nickel is a suspected carcinogen and free-radical catalyst.

Finally, some parting words from the Community Nutrition Institute, which reprinted an indictment of margarine and hydrogenation from the "*Entrophy Institute Review*" of Ontario, Canada, in 1980:

> If governments really wanted to do something positive for the arteries of North America, they would ban outright the sale of all products containing trans fatty acids. The margarine, vegetable shortening and salad oil makers for too long have used the cholesterol bogeyman to scare people, all the while slipping them the phony trans acids....
>
> The industry could, in fact, make other molecular misfits for an extra cost of two cents a pound, but they have not bothered, preferring to spend money on advertising the health benefits of their

sloppily made polyunsaturates. The sale of these products represents a gross failure, the result of a lack of social responsibility on the part of the industry, a disinterested medical research community, and a compliant government. Such indifference and irresponsibility are not tolerated in Germany, where the population demands and gets trans-free (less than 1%) products.

Are you interested in a margarine substitute? I suggest butter.

7

THE MONOUNSATURATES AND SATURATES AMONG US

*Don't plant an olive tree if
only your grandchildren are to enjoy it.*
—PEASANT PROVERB

The Monounsaturates

There is good news for food lovers because three of the tastiest cooking oils of all are on the healthy fat list. These are olive, peanut, and avocado oils. Called mono-unsaturated oils, these oils are more stable at high temperatures and less prone to oxidation than their sister polyunsaturates. The Greeks and Italians have been consuming olive oil for centuries and are known for their low incidence of heart disease.

Produced in California and in countries all over the world, including Portugal, Spain, France, Greece, Italy, Tunisia, and Morocco, olive oil is graded into three categories, which are determined by the method of extraction. These three grades are extra virgin, virgin, and pure. The first two (extra virgin and virgin) can truly be labeled "cold processed" because the hand or hydraulic presses used for extraction generate no heat. Extra virgin, which is the most expensive and ranges from a light green to deep green color, is made with the choicest olives from the first pressing. Virgin oil, similar in color and aroma, is also made from the first pressing but uses a lower-quality olive. Pure olive oil is a combination of refined oils from later pressings.

Research by Dr. Scott M. Grundy, director of the University of Texas Health Sciences Center, has promoted the health value of monounsaturates in the diet. His report in the *New England Journal of Medicine*, March 1986, showed that the monounsaturate type of fatty acid found in olive and peanut oils was more successful at protecting arteries from clogging cholesterol than a low-fat, high-carbohydrate diet. In order to avoid saturated fats—the fat found in butter, cheese, and red meat, for example—people have been turning to carbohydrates, as found in Pritikin-style diets, and/or using polyunsaturated oils from corn and safflower. Now the newly identified healthy fats made from olive and peanut oils give a palatable alternative to the bland, low-fat diets that doctors, dietitians, and nutritionists have been promoting for years.

For health-conscious cooks, the olive and peanut oils produce wonderful culinary results. They make richly satisfying salad dressings and stir sautés. They can also be used in the preparation of baked goods. Peanut oil, because of its milder flavor, is preferred in the making of bread. A word of caution is in order, though. The olive oil is a solid healthy-fat choice because of its long-term track record of healthful use by the peoples of the Mediterranean Basin. Peanut oil does not yet have the same reputation in modern medical circles. Animal tests have shown it to be an artery-clogging substance, and peanuts are high in arachidonic acid, which is connected to inflammatory prostaglandins. It would be wise to emphasize olive oil until peanut oil has been completely exonerated.

Enter Canola Oil

A newcomer to the monounsaturated oils is canola oil sold in supermarkets and health food stores. Canola oil is second only to olive oil in its percentage of mono-unsaturated fat (62% in canola vs. 77% in olive oil). Derived from rapeseed—a plant seed like the mustard seed—canola is versatile because it is practically flavorless. It is the perfect choice for cutting the full-bodied flavor of olive oil when used half and half.

The Saturates

While the monounsaturated fats are the current dietary heroes of America, the saturated fats are considered current dietary villains. Called saturated fats because the carbon chains are completely filled with hydrogen atoms, these fats are found in animal foods such as red meats and dairy products, and in vegetable oils such as coconut, palm, and palm kernel. Because they raise serum cholesterol more than do the polyunsaturates, they are considered almost poisonous. Yet, they perform many necessary functions in the body.

Saturated fats are needed for energy storage, to cushion organs against shock, and to insulate vital tissues against the cold. The body's capacity for energy storage in the form of fat cells is an evolutionary marvel. Over millions of years our bodies have adapted to periodic famine by building up an energy reserve. Nature in her wisdom provides extra protection for women for childbearing and nursing by storing extra reserves (fat) in their buttocks and thighs.

The problem with saturated fats is related more to excessive consumption and to cooking techniques than to the fat itself. The two prime sources of saturated fats in our diet come from fast food restaurants and foods that are frozen or processed. Fast foods are a $5 billion a year business. On a typical day, 45 million people are fast feeding. McDonald's alone has sold some 60 billion hamburgers. In the book *Amazing Facts*, I learned that if all those McBurgers were stacked, they would create a pile twenty times the height of the Sears Tower in

Chicago, the world's tallest building, which is 1,454 feet
tall! The worldwide chain has sold enough milkshakes
to fill every gas tank in America!

Fast Foods

We tend to overeat saturated fats because they are separated from their original food source, such as beef tallow, coconut oil, or palm oil, and are used for commercial
cooking. Because they are more stable against heat and
oxidation than are the polyunsaturates, saturated fats
are used in restaurant food production. They become
hidden in many deep-fat-fried fast foods such as french
fries, onion rings, fish, and chicken. The highly saturated coconut oil is one of the prime ingredients in fast
food shakes and nondairy creamers. Many people don't
realize that the saturated vegetable oils are more saturated than beef fat. The information in the chart below
may prove surprising to many people.

Oil or Fat	Percentage of Saturated Fatty Acids
Coconut oil	92
Palm kernel oil	86
Butterfat	66
Beef tallow	52
Palm oil	51
Lard	41
Cottonseed oil	27

Since the average American eats over one-third of all
meals in restaurants, including fast food chains, we are
being inundated with hidden saturated fats.

In 1986, McDonald's and Burger King yielded to public pressure by switching from beef fat to vegetable oil
for their deep frying. Other chains may follow suit.
While their intentions are good, more damaged fats are

introduced into the American diet in the form of trans fats. The polyunsaturated vegetable oils that McDonald's and Burger King are using are much more easily damaged at the high frying temperatures (350 degrees). The continuous reuse of the same frying oil results in even more trans fats. The oil goes rancid sooner. The original reason for saturated fats for restaurant use was their stability over polyunsaturates.

The problem with saturated fats is twofold: First, their presence biochemically blocks the essential fatty acid conversion into the beneficial prostaglandins. Prostaglandins have been shown to lower blood cholesterol and triglycerides and to promote overall cardiovascular protection by inhibiting blood clots, dilating blood vessels, and lowering blood pressure. By inhibiting prostaglandins, saturated fats promote heart disease. Second, whenever fat is eaten, bile acids are produced by the liver to aid in fat absorption in the intestines. High-fat diets cause too much bile to be produced. When there is insufficient fiber in the diet, bile acids remain in the digestive system for too long and are changed into noxious substances by bacteria. In America, high-fat diets usually go hand-in-hand with low fiber intake.

One of the easier solutions to this problem is simply to avoid all fried foods. Another is to eat more fiber. Fiber-rich foods are vegetables, fruits, legumes (peas and beans), and grains (see Chapter 10, "The Lowdown on Fiber").

Convenience Foods

Fast foods are also convenience foods. Frozen dinners and entrees are extremely popular convenience foods. In 1985 there was a 26 percent increase in the sales of frozen dinners and entrees. This was double the 1982 level. According to the same report by Business Trend Analysts, Inc., retail sales of frozen dinners and entrees were thought to reach $4.5 billion in 1986. Convenience foods are increasing in demand because of more people living alone, the increase of working mothers, smaller families, people living longer, and the emphasis on less time spent on food preparation. The microwave oven has spurred sales in frozen foods. In a 1985 poll of seven hundred working women by *Mademoiselle* magazine regarding their shopping and eating habits, it was revealed that while there is an interest and concern about the nutritional quality of food, most are still not making their meals "from scratch." Sixty percent buy frozen foods; 67 percent buy convenience foods; 38 percent eat them three times per week. Recent surveys show that a majority of Americans eat convenience foods at home. According to the *Nutrition Action Health Letter*, a record 42 percent of meals were eaten away from home in 1983, based on a Gallup survey. Based on these statistics, we can see a strong "tendency" toward turning the responsibility of our food selection and preparation over to total strangers.

However, like their restaurant counterparts, frozen food also means hidden fat. *The average frozen food entree contains over 50 percent fat.* We are forced to ask the question, are we eating frozen food or frozen fat? The chart on page 61 details the fat content of frozen dinners and entrees.

The conclusion from all this is that fast foods are here to stay. Busy lifestyles simply do not allow much time in the kitchen or supermarket anymore.

Is There a Solution?

Our fat problems are directly related to the effects of contemporary technology on the quality of nutrition, and the resultant effects on health and well-being. While we have the technology to process food and still preserve health, what we have done is to produce food that looks and tastes good, and that is profitable and convenient for the manufacturer, but is unhealthy. As long as

Frozen Dinners & Entrées
(Average Over Product Line)

Brand *(serving size)*	Fat *(% of cals)*	Calories	Sodium *(mg)*	Price* *(per lb.)*	
La Choy Dinners (12 oz.)	10	243	1822	na	
Great Escapes Lite (10 oz.)	15	279	1053	$3.58#	
Light & Elegant (9 oz.)	19	259	880	4.62#	
Benihana (na)	20	347	1311	4.03	
Armour Classic Lites (11 oz.)	21	265	954	5.10	LEAN
Lean Cuisine (10 oz.)	28	260	978	4.11	
Mrs. Paul's Light (10 oz.)	29	254	836	5.80	
Green Giant Entrées (10 oz.)	32	347	996	4.15	
Chun King Dinners (12 oz.)	32	334	na	na	
Legume (11 oz.)	33	265	435	5.17	INTERMEDIATE
Weight Watchers (10 oz.)	35	277	1051	4.93	
Armour Dinner Classics (11 oz.)	39	391	1339	5.16	
Celentano (10 oz.)	40	357	672	4.33	
Swanson 4-Part Dinners (12 oz.)	40	483	1154	2.52	
Patio Dinners (13 oz.)	41	618	na	na	
Hungry Man Dinners (17 oz.)	41	728	1772	2.70#	
Hungry Man Entrées (13 oz.)	41	531	1476	na	
Le Menu (11 oz.)	42	398	1001	5.45	
Budget Gourmet (10 oz.)	43	373	849	2.87	
Swift Internat'l Entrées (6 oz.)	43	358	865	na	FATTY
Swanson Entrées (8 oz.)	45	310	908	2.88#	
Banquet American Favorite Dinners (11 oz.)	45	439	1331	1.82#	
Stouffer's Entrées (9 oz.)	46	343	1130	2.56	
Barber Foods (7 oz.)	47	426	957	4.55#	
Banquet Family Entrées (8 oz.)	49	285	989	na	
Old El Paso (na)	55	359	623	4.67	

*Prices obtained in Washington, D.C.
#Average price based on fewer than five items.
na = not available
Source: *Nutrition Action Health Letter*, November 1985.

the public is willing to buy convenience foods that are high in fat and salt and low in fiber, the manufacturers will continue to make them.

I am pleased to report that I am aware of one food company where food processing has been based on good nutrition for over forty years. The company is Walnut Acres, located in Penn's Creek, Pennsylvania. Walnut Acres is a farm that practices organic farming on five hundred acres of chemical-free soil. They use no pesticides or fungicides in their products. They take special care in the processing of their oils to ensure a fresh, nonrancid, nutritious product. They also have a line of foods that is canned and dried without the use of preservatives or additives. They process their own ingredients on the farm in small batches to ensure freshness. Quality control is complete from start to finish. Walnut Acres is the original direct-from-the-farm natural food provider. Farm-fresh foods are produced daily, and pure, untreated mountain water from deep wells is used in food preparation. It is hoped that the example set by Walnut Acres will serve as a model for large-scale food processing in the future.

8

CHOLESTEROL AND THE NEW NUTRITION DIET

There is still some confusion about dietary cholesterol and blood cholesterol. How much cholesterol you eat is not as significant as how much remains in the bloodstream.
—Dr. Ronald Goor,
former official of the National Heart,
Lung and Blood Institute

You might be wondering how cholesterol fits into the New Nutrition Diet picture. Well, cholesterol is a friend, not a foe, when treated properly. The real question, then, is how has it been treated? Most important, has it been damaged by heat or oxygen?

Cholesterol is such an important substance that it is contained in practically every cell in the human body and used for many body functions. It helps the body manufacture adrenal hormones and sex hormones in both males and females. It also aids in manufacturing vitamin D and bile acids, which are used for fat digestion. Much of the brain itself is composed of cholesterol, and it also helps form the insulation around nerves. Cholesterol acts as a lubricant to the artery walls to reduce friction in blood flow. In fact, cholesterol is so vital that the liver will produce it on its own if there is not enough entering the body from dietary sources.

Almost three-fourths of your cholesterol is made by your liver, whereas one-fourth is derived from the foods in your diet.

Cholesterol is found only in animal fats such as chicken, fish, beef, pork, and lamb, and in animal byproducts such as milk, cheese, butter, and eggs. Biologically, no vegetable can contain cholesterol. So, Mazola, Puritan, and other highly promoted vegetable oils aren't proclaiming any unique advantage when they boast that their oil is cholesterol-free. And, while these oils may be truly free of cholesterol, the fact that they are heat treated and refined means they may contain elevated levels of trans fats, which are ineffective in protecting against cardiovascular disease, their advertised role. In fact, these heat-damaged oils may actually hasten cardiovascular disease.

While the oil manufacturers have deactivated the once-beneficial vegetable oils, careless cooking and storage practices in restaurants and on the home front can actually sabotage normally healthful cholesterol foods. According to a 1979 study by Dr. C. B. Taylor in the *American Journal of Nutrition*, oxidized cholesterol from food sources that are left out at room temperature or that are fried, smoked, cured (sausage), or aged (cheese) can be highly atherogenic (plaque producing). It is not pure cholesterol that creates artery-clogging plaque, but rather the toxic substances produced by the oxidation of cholesterol. Oxidized derivatives of cholesterol are unstable and decompose into free radicals, which damage blood vessel walls.

Foods that can cause problems are improperly stored eggs, milk, or butter that are exposed to room temperature for long periods of time and are not stored in tightly sealed containers. Other oxidized cholesterol sources can be found in any fast food fried chicken, fish, and hamburgers. Dried milk, dried eggs, and packaged, dry baking mixes (custards, cakes, puddings, pancakes) are also added to the list. In fact, any animal food that has been exposed to the ravages of oxygen for extended periods of time is likely to contain chemically altered cholesterol. This can be seen in the cooking of eggs. Hard-boiled or fried eggs produce the highest serum cholesterol; scrambled or baked eggs produce less; soft-boiled eggs produce the least.

High-Density Lipoproteins (HDL) and Low-Density Lipoproteins (LDL)

Cholesterol is carried through the bloodstream in two protein fractions, high-density lipoprotein (HDL) and low-density lipoprotein (LDL). The HDL is considered the good cholesterol because it transports cholesterol away from the arterial walls to the liver for disposal, thus blocking its buildup in the blood vessels. The bad cholesterol (LDL) deposits cholesterol in the arterial walls, promoting hardening of the arteries. It is valuable to evaluate both total cholesterol and HDL for the most complete coronary risk assessment. In terms of total cholesterol, the following recommendations are made by the National Institutes of Health. The numbers represent milligrams of cholesterol per deciliter (mg/dl) of blood.

Age	Moderate Risk	High Risk
20–29	greater than 200	greater than 220
30–39	greater than 220	greater than 240
40 +	greater than 240	greater than 260

The ratio between total cholesterol and HDL cholesterol is now considered more important than just the total cholesterol value alone. In addition, there are cholesterol levels which are age-and-sex-dependant that are associated with the increased risk of coronary artery disease. It is interesting to note that women in general have higher average HDL cholesterol levels than do most men (55 mg/dl for women and 45 mg/dl for men). Concurrently, women evidence less coronary heart disease than do males.

A decisive study reported in the *Journal of the American Medical Association* in early 1984, known as the Lipid Research Clinic's Coronary Primary Prevention Trial, demonstrated that elevated cholesterol levels were connected with heart disease risk factors. This ten-year, $150 million study was the largest, most expensive project in medical history. It concluded that elevated cholesterol levels in the bloodstream were a major risk factor in heart disease. When blood cholesterol levels were lowered, the incidence of fatal heart attacks was reduced. The four thousand men who participated in the study and lowered their blood cholesterol values, either through diet or drugs, lowered their incidence of heart disease and heart attacks. Thus, it is now generally suggested that adult Americans lower their total cholesterol value below 200 mg/dl. The American Heart Association states that most heart attacks occur when blood levels reach between 210 and 265 mg/dl. Children should not exceed 185 mg/dl.

Elevated cholesterol levels are commonly found in liver and cardiovascular disease, diabetes, stress, and low thyroid function. Stress cannot be overlooked as an external factor that can upset body chemistry. The emotional stress factor can also raise cholesterol levels independent of diet. It has also been shown that stress management techniques can lower cholesterol levels, independent of diet. Dr. Meyer Friedman, who conceived the notion of the Type A and Type B behavior system, underscores the stress factor in the development of heart disease. Dr. Dean Ornish echoes agreement in his book *Stress, Diet and Your Heart*.

While much attention has been focused on the danger of too much cholesterol in the bloodstream, the danger of too little has been relatively ignored. Levels far below 180 mg/dl have been correlated with anemia, acute infection, and excess thyroid function. Moreover, significantly depressed cholesterol values have been found in autoimmune disorders. Low cholesterol levels may function as a precursor to impaired immunity, although this has not been fully substantiated.

Since high blood cholesterol values can be caused by a number of factors such as age, obesity, stress, and cigarette smoking, it is wise to control these factors as much as possible. Losing weight, managing stress, and stopping cigarette smoking are good preventive measures to reduce major risk factors in the prevention of cardiovascular disease.

The ultimate question is, what is the most effective method of lowering cholesterol in the bloodstream? In terms of diet, major researchers believe that it is not dietary cholesterol that raises blood levels, but excessive saturated fats in the form of red meats and whole-milk dairy products. Dr. Michael White, associate director for Prevention, Education and Control at the National Heart, Lung and Blood Institute, states: "Another point of confusion is in thinking that dietary cholesterol is the main culprit. Actually, saturated fats have a greater effect on blood cholesterol." In agreement, Dr. Bruce McManus of the University of Nebraska Medical Center adds that "... saturated fat intake above a certain level is as important and probably more important than one's intake of cholesterol in determining your blood levels of cholesterol." These conventional experts essentially agree that it is not the cholesterol itself in foods that creates a high serum level in the bloodstream. Fat is more the problem.

Ever since cholesterol was identified in the 1960s as a component of the fatty deposits found in the inner walls of the arteries, it has been thought that cholesterol was the main culprit in coronary artery disease. However, it was never proved that it was cholesterol that caused the plaque formation in the first place. In the case of cholesterol, association is not necessarily causation. In other words, the presence of cholesterol may be the result of the disease, not necessarily the cause.

Dr. Henry Bieler was the nutritional mentor of actress Gloria Swanson. While she was at the Pritikin Center, she introduced me to Bieler's writings. He defies current convention with his visionary theory about the way in which cholesterol works in the body. In studying Bieler's ideas, I concluded that so much unfavorable publicity has been unjustly directed toward cholesterol that the following passage from Dr. Bieler's book *Food Is Your Best Medicine* is important in clarifying the issue:

> During the development of the embryo, cholesterol is supplied by the mother's blood. After birth the child must manufacture its own. The oil needed for this, nature supplies in the most useful fat, cream, otherwise known as butterfat. One of the important functions of the liver is the synthesis of cholesterol from butterfat. Of course, other vegetable and animal fats can be used, but during the child's early development, butterfat is supplied by mother's milk.
>
> The cholesterol, built up by the liver cells from simple fats, circulates in the blood in just the proper concentration to be utilized by the cells which line the artery walls, and is held there as the perfect lubricant. As these cells wear out, they are cast off, together with their cholesterol, and excreted by the body, while new cells grow and absorb new cholesterol from the blood. Thus, there occurs a continuous in-and-out flow of cholesterol, which, as long as the body is in perfect health, is maintained at a specific level.
>
> When the physiological level for the cholesterol is disturbed by a more rapid breaking-down than building-up process, the overall cholesterol concentration in the blood is increased and there occurs a state of *hypercholestremia*, i.e., too much cholesterol in the blood. There are simple laboratory tests by which the amount of circulating cholesterol can be determined.

The only condition that can cause a more rapid breaking-down than building-up of cholesterol is a diseased state of the artery walls. *Overeating of fats and oils, as long as they are in their natural state, cannot cause arterial disease.* The body merely stores the excess as fat.

It is only when "unnatural" fats, or "natural" fats which have been altered by being overheated, are consumed as food that the trouble arises. Especially is the composition of the fat altered when it is heated with starch (for example, French-fried potatoes). I have found that it is impossible for the liver to synthesize a perfect cholesterol from a fat that has been heated with starch. The resulting cholesterol is used by the body for arterial lining, but being an unnatural or altered cholesterol, it fails to wear well, soon breaks down and is corroded, resulting in various forms of arterial disease and degeneration—arteriosclerosis (commonly called hardening or narrowing of the artery walls, which causes them to lose their elasticity); atherosclerosis (fatty deposits on the arterial walls, which may impede or even block the blood flow); coronary thrombosis (blood clotting in the arteries, which blocks the blood supply to the heart); and aneurism (ruptured tumor in the artery wall). In these states the concentration of cholesterol in the blood is much higher than the normal level. The increased level can be detected early by the alert physician as a danger signal which will lead him to make a study of the patient's fat metabolism.*

According to Bieler, elevated serum levels of cholesterol suggest a problem in fat metabolism caused by damaged fats that the body cannot process. Elevated blood levels of cholesterol are not related to a diet high in saturates unless those fats are overheated.

---

*Henry G. Bieler, M.D. *Food Is Your Best Medicine* (New York: Ballantine Books, 1984) pp. 114–115.

Bieler does not specifically discriminate between heat-damaged saturated fats and polyunsaturated fats. The fact is that polyunsaturates are much more easily damaged by heat and oxidation. Rancid polyunsaturates generate free radicals, which attack the blood vessel walls. The free radicals also stimulate the production of inflammatory prostaglandins. As we've already seen, the trans-fat content of heat-damaged oils suppresses the production of antiinflammatory prostaglandins, and inflammation becomes chronic. Cholesterol synthesis is increased during inflammation, and it is drawn to the damaged blood vessel walls. The accumulated cholesterol actually protects the damaged blood vessels like a bandage on a wound.

At first it may seem that these different views of fat and health are quite divergent. But they are actually related. It is easy to blame fats in general when it is heat-damaged fats that are the real problem. In the high-fat American diet, higher saturated-fat intake is generally associated with heat-damaged and oxidized fats. Witness the popularity of fast foods and the reuse of frying oils. While studies have linked fat to heart disease, diabetes, and cancer of the breast, colon, and prostate, they have not attempted to determine whether the damage caused by heat, hydrogenation, oxygen, or homogenization is actually responsible.

Likewise, it is easy to blame fats in general when it is heat-damaged polyunsaturates that are the real source of the problem. Because polyunsaturates are more susceptible to oxygen than are saturated fats, they go rancid more quickly. Polyunsaturates are therefore proportionately more responsible for the disease-causing activity of fat. The peroxides formed by rancidity attack cell membranes, enzymes, and DNA. They are responsible for premature aging, skin wrinkling, heart disease, and cancer.

Heat-damaged and hydrogenated polyunsaturates also form trans fats, which have been associated with the same diseases as fats (or heat-damaged fats) have been connected with. Trans fats inhibit beneficial prostaglandin activity and cause chronic inflammation. Trans fats worsen all diseases, accelerating the degenerative processes initiated by rancid fats.

Thus, disease is not the result of cholesterol, saturated fats, or polyunsaturated fats; it's a result of what's been done to them. The destructive effects of heat, hydrogenation, oxygen, and homogenization can affect all of these food constituents. Cholesterol can become oxidized and stale; excessive saturated fats from fast foods and convenience foods can clog the system and block prostaglandin production. Polyunsaturates can become rancid and form free radicals. In these damaged or unbalanced states, these foods cause disease. Unprocessed and taken in moderation, they provide needed nutrition.

Triglycerides

Any discussion of cholesterol would be incomplete without including the triglycerides. Basically the word *triglyceride* can be used interchangeably with *fat* or *oil*. Triglyceride is also the form in which the body stores fat in the connective tissue. That roll above your stomach, for instance, is actually excess triglyceride. In terms of diet, too much refined carbohydrates in the form of white sugar, white flour, and products such as white bread, cakes, cookies, candies, and soda, as well as alcohol, can account for elevation of blood triglyceride levels. Even too much fruit and natural unsweetened fruit juice can elevate triglyceride levels.

Although I am not aware of any clinical studies, I have observed that people who drink more than two cups of coffee per day have difficulty in reducing elevated triglyceride levels. Levels between 70 and 150 mg of triglyceride per deciliter of blood are considered optimally healthy by most nutritionally oriented physicians. A low triglyceride value, like a low cholesterol value,

is not necessarily a sign of better health. When triglyceride values are lower than 70 mg, it may indicate that
fatty acids are not being released properly into the
bloodstream and there is some low-grade liver dysfunction. Conversely, when triglyceride levels are much greater
than 150 mg, it may reflect a diet too high in processed
foods or fruits, or a liver problem in which fatty acids
are being poorly broken down and utilized in the
bloodstream.

During my years at the Pritikin Center, I noted that
the excessive use of apple juice concentrate used as a
sweetener to replace all forms of sugar including honey
in many of the Center's recipes contributed to high
triglyceride levels. Diets that emphasize high amounts
of carrot juice or fruits of any kind can induce unusually high triglyceride levels. Excessive sugar in the diet
from refined sugar or fruit sources can be stored in the
tissues as excess fat.

9

THE NEW NUTRITION DIET FOOD CHOICES: WHERE THE ESSENTIAL FATS ARE FOUND

Adequate food is the ...
laboratory of long life.
—DR. CHARLES MAYO

Foods or food supplements that are rich sources of essential fats must be included in the daily diet. The essential fats are required for prostaglandins, which are intimately involved with every cell of the body. Since prostaglandins are destroyed as soon as they perform their duties, a daily supply of essential-fat raw material is necessary to continue the prostaglandin health watch and control. For most people, two tablespoons of essential fat per day is all that is required.

Essential fat is also crucial during the initial weight loss period in order to enable the body to burn calories more efficiently. It is also important after weight is lost to maintain efficient burning of calories.

While unrefined oils or GLA supplements can help nourish the brown fat I call your fat burner, the Omega-3 rich foods, or EPA supplements, can protect your entire cardiovascular system. In addition to aiding in weight loss and maintaining healthy arteries, eating essential fat foods may alleviate food allergies and depression and strengthen hair and brittle nails.

The GLA Fat Burners

These food sources supply the highest amounts of cis-linoleic acid, which can convert to gamma-linolenic acid in your body:

Unrefined Vegetable Oil	Percentages of Linoleic Acid
Safflower	78
Sunflower	69
Corn	62
Soy	61
Walnut	59
Cottonseed	54
Sesame	43
Rice bran	32
Peanut	31
Olive	15
Coconut	2

Other sources of cis-linoleic acid include green leafy vegetables such as kale, collard greens and swiss chard, raw nuts and seeds, liver, kidneys, brains, sweetbreads, and lean red meats.

Other direct sources of GLA come from plants. The richest source is borage, at 24 percent GLA. Next is black currant oil at 15 to 19 percent GLA, then gooseberry oil at 10 to 12 percent GLA, and last, evening primrose oil at 2 to 9 percent GLA, depending on the strength of the plant.

Although black currant oil is rapidly gaining popularity on the market, it is not a wise choice for GLA supplementation because it contains a potent GLA inhibitor.

Omega-3s

There is a great variety of essential fat available with the EPA omega-3 food group. Many cold-water fish and seafoods contain sufficiently high amounts of EPA for optimum cardiovascular benefit. The highest concentrations of EPA have been found in north Atlantic sardine oil at 18 percent EPA, while salmon oil contains 9 percent and mackerel oil has about 5 percent. In general, the fattier the fish, the more omega-3 it contains.

The following chart shows the highest EPA content of selected fish:

Comparison of EPA Content in 3.5 Ounce Servings of Selected Fish

Fish	Milligrams of EPA
Anchovy	747
Salmon, chinook	633
Herring	606
Mackerel	585
Tuna, albacore	337
Halibut, Pacific	194
Cod, Atlantic	93
Trout, rainbow	84
Haddock	72
Swordfish	30
Red snapper	19
Sole	10

The original producers of EPA are the sea vegetation, or plankton, that inhabit Arctic and Antarctic waters. Next in the food chain are krill (shrimplike organisms), which are eaten by the bigger fish. The production of EPA is actually an antifreeze survival mechanism in extremely cold water temperatures. The colder the water, the more EPA is produced. In warmer waters, little EPA is made by plankton.

Besides fresh edible sea vegetation (EPA disappears if

the seaweed is dried) and fatty fish itself, land-grown green leafy vegetables are another source. Wheat sprouts, wheat germ, nuts and seeds such as walnuts, linseeds, flaxseeds, and soybeans are sources of the EPA precursor, alpha-linolenic acid (ALA). These food sources should not be taken in combination with any other GLA-producing food or supplement, as they will inhibit the GLA prostaglandins. Taken alone, they can enhance EPA prostaglandin production.

The only natural direct source of both GLA and EPA is found in mother's milk, whereas cow's milk is a comparatively low source. When babies were fed skim milk preparations, their appetites dramatically increased and they consumed twice the amount of formula than infants fed on mother's milk, which is naturally high in essential fatty acids. When these infants were put back on a diet of mother's milk, their appetites normalized.

This indicates that appetite control may be naturally regulated with the proper dietary fats. For years doctors have suggested breast-feeding to ensure in children a strong immune system and freedom from allergies. Now we know that GLA and EPA may be the key ingredients in breast milk that are responsible for the healthier breast-fed babies.

For those mothers unable to breast-feed, there is an easy alternative. Essential fatty acids can be absorbed through the skin. You can puncture a GLA capsule, for example, squeeze out the oil quickly to avoid oxidation, and rub it into the baby's abdomen and arms. When the infant is 1 year old and is eating solid foods, the capsule can be opened and mixed with the food.

Essential Fat Dietary Supplements

Encapsulated oils may be the only way for you to include essential fats in your diet if you eat out frequently or eat ready-made frozen foods at home and don't like fish. If these oils are so lacking in the normal diet, then an essential fat in supplement form should be considered a food, not a pill.

Restaurants use either processed heat-treated vegetable oils or hydrogenated vegetable margarines, or both. These substances have no biological value to you and can even thwart GLA utilization in your body. So, while it may be ideal to avoid all of these damaged, unnatural fats, it is really practical to supplement with essential fat to make sure your tissues are properly nourished. It is not enough just to avoid the bad; you still must supplement with the good. When the New Nutrition Diet food choices are limited or unavailable, even at home, these supplements offer fat-burning/calorie-processing power.

Caveat Emptor: What the Buyer Should Know About Fish Oil Capsules

Since the fattier fish are the only significant sources of EPA, many individuals will want to supplement their diets with fish oil capsules. What's wrong with eating fresh fish, you say? First of all, people may not want to eat enough of the fatty fish per day to derive the EPA benefits. Second, the higher the fat content in the fish, the more fat-soluble pollutants that can accumulate. This means that the highest EPA-containing fish may also be high in PCBs (polychlorinated biphenyls) and heavy metals such as mercury and arsenic.

If you choose to go the fish oil capsule route, there are several ways to assess the purity and freshness of the oil brands. The first is taste. High-quality, pure oils do not taste fishy. Fresh oils are mild and sweet-tasting; rancid oils are strongly acrid and bitter. At home you can periodically puncture a capsule and squeeze a drop of oil onto your tongue to check out the taste. The color and clarity are also indications of freshness. As the oils age, they darken and become cloudy. A light color to the oil also assures the removal of the PCBs and heavy metals.

The "freezer test" is a good way to assess the EPA content of fish oils. Put a capsule in the freezer; if it congeals within a few hours, there is a high saturated-fat content. The higher the saturated-fat content, the lower the EPA.

BioSyn is a company that upholds the highest standards of both purity and freshness. Their encapsulated oils are high in essential fats, contaminant free and cholesterol free. The following products and recommended dosages are suggested to derive optimum GLA and EPA benefit. Human breast milk, the only source of both GLA and EPA, is used as the model to determine the ideal maximum intake. Researchers agree that an optimum daily intake for prevention of disease can be up to 850 mg. EPA and 200 mg. GLA (with more GLA for specific weight loss). This information is derived from the fatty acid composition of human breast milk.

Product Name	Recommended Dosage
Omega Syn™ (EPA and GLA)	480 mg. (EPA) and 120 mg. (GLA)
	4 per meal, 2 times daily
For Weight Loss:	4 daily
Gamma 20™ (GLA)	90 mg.
	2 per meal, 2 times daily
EFA Enhance™	Beta carotene, vitamins E, C, B-3, B-6, magnesium, zinc, selenium
	1 per meal, 3 times daily

To order, call toll-free: (800) 346-2703 from 9 A.M. to 5 P.M. E.S.T. Massachusetts residents can call (617) 631-9794 from 9 A.M. to 5 P.M. E.S.T.

Additional Fat Fighters

There are other vitamins that lower abnormally high fat levels, while others protect the essential fats from oxidation. The fat-emulsifying substance lecithin, found in unprocessed vegetable oils and in soy products, is high in choline and inositol. These vitamins in their isolated forms can also produce lecithin in the liver. Total cholesterol values, LDL cholesterol, and triglycerides have been normalized with lecithin. Both niacin and vitamin C have been found to lower cholesterol levels in several clinical studies. Niacin is good for circulation and is a well-known blood vessel dilator. Vitamin C is a general overall blood vessel protector, which also supports the conversion of essential fatty acids into helpful prostaglandins. The English physician Constance Spittle has suggested that atherosclerosis results from long-term vitamin C deficiency, which allows cholesterol to accumulate in the artery walls.

The latest nutritional strategy for combatting abnormally high fat in the blood is the nonessential amino acid L-carnitine. It is considered an effective fat burner because it transfers fatty acids into the mitochondria and can lower cholesterol while elevating the good HDLs. It is directly related to the function of the heart muscle and is deficient in damaged heart tissues.

Cell Defense

The trace minerals selenium and zinc, as well as beta carotene and vitamins C and E, act as antioxidants to help protect vital tissues from the ravages of free radicals. Free radicals, you will remember, are produced by normal metabolic processes, as well as from exposure to radiation and to chemical carcinogens. Free radicals will attack sensitive cell membranes in DNA, causing a host of degenerative diseases. Antioxidants protect against these diseases by scavenging free radicals before they have a chance to do damage. These protective nutrients are found in whole grains, citrus fruits, and green leafy and deep yellow vegetables. The cruciferous family of cabbage, turnips, cauliflower, broccoli, and brussels sprouts are high in another cancer-combating family of substances called indoles.

Vitamin B-6 has supernutrient status as a fat metabolizer and heart disease preventive. Dr. Kilmer McCully, formerly of the Harvard Medical School, believes that B-6 can block the original injury to the arterial lining caused by the toxic amino acid homocysteine. Vitamin B-6 neutralizes the damaging homocysteine into a nontoxic substance that the body can safely utilize. Foods that are recommended vitamin B-6 sources include bananas, carrots, onion, kale, sweet potatoes, asparagus, cauliflower, turnip greens, lentils, peas, and brewer's yeast.

Garlic and Onions

Here are two popular vegetables that benefit lipid metabolism and are versatile favorites in the kitchen. Practically every cuisine in the world makes use of the food-enhancing and medicinal qualities of garlic and onions.

Garlic has been used since antiquity for its healing benefits. During the Middle Ages its medicinal value was prized against killer plagues. As recently as World War II, it was used against typhus and dysentery. Garlic's strong germicidal and strengthening actions have been recognized far into the twentieth century. It is very helpful against yeast-fungus–related disorders. Dr. Michael J. Wargovich of the Anderson Hospital and Tumor Institute in Houston, Texas, reports that garlic oil may inhibit cancer growth in test animals.

The active substance in garlic is a volatile oil called allicin, which has antibacterial and antifungal properties. Allicin is what gives garlic its unmistakable smell. Allicin has been shown to be active against harmful bacteria without affecting friendly bacteria. In laboratory culture studies, garlic has inhibited the growth of the fungi *Candida albicans* and *Aspergillus niger*, two yeasts that affect many allergic individuals.

Besides allicin, garlic also contains vitamins, and the trace minerals vanadium and selenium (a potent antioxidant). Garlic's benefits have been known to help a wide range of human maladies. High blood pressure, cardiovascular disease, intestinal problems, liver trouble, and sinus conditions have all benefited from its use.

In the late 1960s, doctors began studying the fat-cutting properties of garlic. It proved to be a good food in combating high cholesterol and triglyceride levels. Clinical studies demonstrated its effectiveness in reducing platelet aggregation by cutting the stickiness of platelets, thereby reducing the tendency of blood to clot and preventing loss of blood flow through the arterial system. Garlic's numerous benefits in coronary artery disease are becoming well known.

Not to be overlooked, the lowly onion has also proved its worth in protecting the artery walls from blood clots and plaque buildup. The work of Dr. Victor Gurewich, professor of medicine at Tufts University and director of the vascular laboratory at St. Elizabeth's Hospital in Boston, has demonstrated that the juice of one yellow or white onion per day can dramatically raise the beneficial HDL cholesterol levels in the blood. The milder red onions seem not to have the same effect as the more pungent yellow or white varieties. Another prominent researcher, Dr. Arun Bordia, has lowered blood fats in coronary heart disease patients with both onions and garlic.

In cooking, garlic enjoys the distinction of being the second most used condiment in America (black pepper is the first). We love its flavoring in a wide variety of dishes from soups to salads to main courses. There are entire cookbooks devoted to garlic alone, and every year in Gilroy, California, there is a world renowned garlic festival in which new and more innovative ways of eating the venerable "stinking rose" are created.

Studies of the onion show that cooking reduces its cholesterol-controlling ability. The same may apply to garlic. This is why you may want to use raw garlic and

onion in capsule form for their full fat-fighting and
therapeutic benefits. Odorless garlic capsules are available, but not all of them contain allicin. Make sure the
allicin content is verified on the label.

10

THE LOWDOWN ON FIBER

Fiber can make you free.
—JERRY VAN AMERONGEN
cartoonist

Fiber is the indigestible part of plant foods that we used to call "bulk" or "roughage." Because fiber is indigestible, it has no direct nutritional value, but it does have nutritional effects. Like essential fat, fiber gives the dieter a full feeling and many attendant health benefits. When fiber absorbs water and wells up in the intestines, you feel full and therefore satisfied with fewer calories. Other health bonuses from dietary fiber are a steady blood sugar level, cholesterol regulation, and better bowel elimination. These effects depend on the type of fiber eaten.

Dietary fiber can be divided into two types, soluble and insoluble. The water-soluble fibers from fruits, vegetables, peas, beans, and oats are rich in pectins and gums that slow down carbohydrate absorption, which stabilizes blood sugar levels. They are also believed to surround cholesterol molecules with a gellike coating that inhibits cholesterol absorption into the bloodstream. Water-soluble fibers may help to slow down digestion enough to enable the fat-digesting enzyme lipase to further break down fats before they are absorbed.

Insoluble fibers, from wheat bran, whole grains, and beans, assist in elimination. While they don't break down in water, they absorb water in the digestive tract, allowing waste materials to move out (transit) at a faster pace. Insoluble fiber is helpful in bowel disorders such as constipation and diverticular disease, in which weakened areas of the intestinal wall become inflamed. It may also protect against colon cancer by removing fat-soluble carcinogens. When fats and oils are eaten, the liver produces bile acids to break them down for further digestion in the intestines. Bile acids can become cancer causing if they remain in contact with the intestinal walls for too long. Fiber speeds up transit time so that noxious wastes are removed from the system quickly.

However, due to its coarseness, too much insoluble fiber may irritate the bowel—a problem not seen with the softer water-soluble fiber. Another problem with grain fiber, especially wheat bran, is that it can interfere with the absorption of minerals such as calcium, magnesium, iron, and zinc.

Here is a handy guide to finding the soluble fiber that works for you:

Where to Find Soluble Fiber

Food	Serving	Soluble Fiber (g)
GRAINS		
Oat bran	⅓ cup dry	2.0
All-Bran	⅓ cup	1.7
Oat bran muffin	1	1.6
Oatmeal	¾ cup, cooked	1.4
Rye bread	2 slices	0.6
Whole wheat bread	2 slices	0.5
DRIED BEANS & PEAS		
Black-eyed peas	½ cup, cooked	3.7
Kidney beans	½ cup, cooked	2.5
Pinto beans	½ cup, cooked	2.3
Navy beans	½ cup, cooked	2.3
Lentils	½ cup, cooked	1.7
Split peas	½ cup, cooked	1.7

VEGETABLES

Peas	½ cup, canned	2.7
Corn	½ cup, cooked	1.7
Sweet potato	1 baked	1.3
Zucchini	½ cup, cooked	1.3
Cauliflower	½ cup, cooked	1.3
Broccoli	½ cup, cooked	0.9

FRUIT

Prunes	4	1.9
Pear	1	1.1
Apple	1	0.9
Banana	1	0.8
Orange	1	0.7

Source: Personal communication, Janet Tietyen, Research Dietician with Dr. James Anderson, University of Kentucky Medical Center.
Note: Researchers are still perfecting methods of analyzing the total and soluble fiber content of foods. These values may differ from Anderson's earlier values and those of other researchers.
Source: *Nutrition Action Health Letter*, December 1985.

Oat bran, which also contains very small amounts of GLA, is the hottest new water-soluble fiber these days. Studies conducted by Dr. James Anderson, chief of endocrinology at the University of Kentucky Medical Center, show that a regimen of oat bran reduced cholesterol levels by an average of 19 percent in a three-week period. The addition of oat bran, pectin, psyllium seed husks, and guar gum (a fiber from beans) have all proved helpful in lowering blood cholesterol levels in other clinical studies. Oat bran, however, is one of the easiest fiber sources to add to the diet. Because of its cholesterol-fighting ability, oat bran is a welcome addition to the diet of those with high serum cholesterol levels. It can be used as a breakfast cereal, a food thickener, or sprinkled over foods at any time of the day.

Dr. Denis Burkitt, a British surgeon who spent twenty years in Africa, is the pioneer of fiber research. While in Uganda, he observed that heart disease and cancer are virtually nonexistent among the rural Africans. Those who ate a coarse and fiber-full diet did not suffer, as do Americans, the diseases of constipation, hiatal hernia, and varicose veins. The Africans average a total of 25 grams of fiber per day, and with this increased bulk their stools have a shorter bowel transit time—approximately thirty hours instead of the seventy hours or more for the average American. A shorter transit time, as previously explained, means less time for bile wastes to decompose into toxic substances. Bacterial putrefaction is also minimized.

The average American diet contains about 10 grams of fiber. Levels of 25 to 40 grams would be more advisable for cleaner intestines, reduced hunger, and colon cancer prevention. High blood fats, as well as adult-onset diabetes, can also be managed by a high-fiber diet. Fiber slows down absorption of nutrients from the intestinal tract, resulting in more stable levels of blood sugar.

It is not necessary to count fiber grams as long as you are eating unrefined, unprocessed foods. Brown rice, for example, contains three times as much fiber as white rice; and a raw apple has twice as much fiber as an equivalent amount of applesauce. High-fiber foods such as beans, grains, and vegetables are rich in complex carbohydrates and are part of the New Nutrition Diet.

Recognizing the fiber dilemma of modernday America, international food scientist Dr. Arnold Spicer, a contemporary of Dr. Denis Burkitt, has created a fiber-rich diet food. This food, called NutriWheat, contains 6 grams of fiber and is made with a special patented formula that enables the fiber to expand to a volume five times greater than the natural volume of wheat. The expansion technique breaks down the gluten component of the wheat, which allows those individuals with gluten sensitivities to enjoy NutriWheat without the digestive difficulty that often accompanies other wheat-based foods.

The expanded NutriWheat, enjoyed as a complete food in itself, absorbs liquids and expands the muscle lining of the stomach so that hunger is delayed. Satiety is reached with as little as 100 calories per bag because of this process. Although NutriWheat contains corn oil, the corn oil is not heated during the processing of the food. The oil is also protected from oxidation by a special packaging material. Considering these factors, the production is more nutritionally sound than most other snack foods on the market.

The technology to create high-fiber snack foods has already been developed. Like Walnut Acres in total food processing, Spicer's International is a forerunner in nutritious convenience foods. (To obtain NutriWheat see page 128 for address and toll free number.)

11

NEW LIGHT ON FITNESS

*Few seem conscious that there is such
a thing as physical morality.*
—HIPPOCRATES

Any diet book worth its weight (loss) has to consider exercise as a way to burn additional calories. This part of the New Nutrition Diet plan may well be the easiest part to follow. There are really no excuses in this area because the exercise prescription stays away from taxing anatomical activity such as jogging or heavy workouts. Instead, the preferred exercises are dancing, swimming, cycling, and walking, with walking the Number One choice. Remember, though, to consult with your physician before beginning any exercise program.

The important aspect these three forms of exercise have in common is that they are all aerobic. Exercise that increases the body's use of oxygen is considered aerobic. The benefits from aerobic exercise include:

- Conditioning of heart, lungs, and blood vessels
- Firming and toning of muscles
- Increased coordination and flexibility of joints
- Improvements in circulation and general endurance

Medical research has shown that individuals who are more active suffer fewer heart attacks. They are also more likely to survive a heart attack. The *Journal of the American Medical Association* has reported that with regular aerobic exercise, high blood pressure can be reduced in mildly hypertensive people. Because modern lifestyles have made us increasingly sedentary, we need to schedule our exercise on a regular basis.

It is important to include some form of aerobic activity at least three to five times a week for a period of 20 to 30 minutes. To make sure your exercise is effective, it is wise to check your target heart rate (THR). Reaching your THR for at least 20 minutes is a goal of aerobic exercise.

To calculate your maximum heart rate, subtract your age from 220. Your target heart rate is 65 percent to 85 percent of your maximum heart rate. For example, if you are 40 years old, your maximum heart rate would be 180 (220 − 40 = 180). Your low-end THR is 127 (65 percent of 180) and your high-end THR is 153 (85 percent of 180). When beginning an exercise program, start at the lower value and work up slowly. It is important to allow the heart muscle time to strengthen and adjust to each increase in heart rate. In overweight and unconditioned individuals, this may take as long as two years.

To measure your heart rate, take your pulse on your wrist or neck immediately after at least 20 minutes of exercise. Count for 15 seconds and multiply by 4. For example, if you count 32 heartbeats in 15 seconds, your heart rate is 128 beats per minute. This is well within the boundaries of your target heart rate.

It is important to remember that muscle tissue burns more energy than fat tissue. The greater the amount of muscle tissue, the higher the metabolic rate. A further bonus of exercise is that it affects body metabolism for up to fifteen hours after you stop doing the exercise itself. Exercise can also suppress appetite for several hours. If you exercise before dinner you will eat less and relieve the tension that builds up during the day.

Walking is your best bet because, of all the sports, it is most easily accessible to most people at most times of the year. Walking is preferred over running because running imposes a great deal of stress on the knees and skeletal system. Injuries to joints and tendons are common because with each stride while running, the impact is increased to four times the body's weight. In women, this impact can have devastating effects on the fragile pelvic bones, especially in postmenopausal women (with tendencies toward osteoporosis).

Brisk, vigorous walking burns just as many calories per mile as does running. It may even provide better muscle toning than running because, when walking a mile, more steps are taken than when running a mile.

So walk wherever and whenever you can. The only other requirement is that walking be done outside during the daytime. Natural light, like essential fat, is an endangered nutrient in which many of us are deficient. We spend too much time indoors under incandescent and fluorescent lights that prevent natural full-spectrum light from entering our eyes. Even the glass in our office windows, automobiles, eyeglasses, and contact lenses blocks the beneficial ultraviolet rays from natural daylight. Light entering the eyes influences the master glands, such as the pineal, which influences mood and behavior, and the pituitary, which controls all the other glands of the endocrine system. We need the entire full spectrum of natural sunlight for complete health. Inadequate exposure to natural illumination can induce a form of depression known as "seasonal affective disorder" (SAD). SAD has been shown to result from diminished exposure to natural light as the days grow shorter.

You should walk briskly for at least 30 minutes outside, without sunglasses, regular glasses, or contact lenses if possible to allow the sunlight to reach the retina of the eye. When walking, get your heart pumping at your target heart rate and try to maintain that pace for 20 minutes. If you are in an office and can't exercise during working hours, try to take some of your lunch or coffee breaks outside in the sun, and take off your glasses!

Dancing is another good exercise. The low-impact aerobic dancing, square dancing, and fast-moving ballroom dancing are all enjoyable and fun. Home exercise videotapes now feature low-intensity workouts that are also good movers. More important, they are safer for people who are out of shape or overweight than the earlier high-intensity type because they are paced and build endurance slowly but surely.

Swimming is a very popular and recommended exercise. Because the body weight is suspended in water, every muscle in the body can be exercised without strain. To really condition the muscles, you might try poolwalking. At the shallow end of the pool, walk from one side to the other, which has the effect of dragging the legs through the water. This provides a beneficial workout for all the leg muscles.

Bicycling is also a beneficial body conditioner. Outside, for full-spectrum light, and out of traffic, for full-spectrum safety, bicycling provides good cardiovascular exercise. The bicycle seat should be as high as possible while still keeping your knees slightly bent at full extension. The gears should be as low as possible to enable easy, rapid pedaling. If you climb a lot of hills, use the low gears on a ten-speed bike. If you use a stationary bike, take it outdoors or put it in front of an open window where sunlight can reach your eyes.

Of course, there are many other suitable aerobic exercises that stimulate the heart and burn calories. By all means, if your favorite activity is tennis, racquet ball, skipping rope, rowing, cross-country skiing, roller skating, or even stair climbing, then continue it on a regular basis. Whenever you enjoy what you do, you are more likely to continue to do it.

Information on exercise and fitness can be obtained toll free by calling The Aerobics Center at (800) 527-0362, 8:00 A.M. to 4:30 P.M. C.S.T.

12

CHEMISTRY IN THE KITCHEN

Most health problems begin in the kitchen.
—PAUL DUDLEY WHITE, M.D.

Now it's time to turn to the practical issues. That is, what you should eat and how the food should be prepared for optimum health. Let's review and summarize some basic tenets of the New Nutrition Diet. Here are the Prime Contenders:

Prime Contenders

- **Expeller-pressed crude or unrefined oils**

  For salad: Safflower, sunflower, sesame, corn, walnut, almond, hazelnut, peanut, canola oil, extra virgin olive, and virgin olive.

  For cooking: Peanut, canola oil, extra virgin and virgin olive.

Note: Shelled raw nuts and seeds from which the above are derived are not a reliable good-fat source because they are generally rancid from exposure to heat, air, and light. They are best bought unshelled in the raw state and then "home toasted" before eating. Commercially roasted nuts have been heated at excessively high temperatures, which hastens rancidity. More information about how to purchase, store, and prepare these foods is included under "Desirable Cooking Methods," p. 107, and "Stocking and

Storing the Staples," p. 120. I suggest that nuts and seeds be used primarily as condiments.

Sesame seed butter is an unusually stable nut butter that resists rancidity. It is particularly high in calcium and the two amino acids methionine and tryptophan, which are usually deficient in most vegetable proteins.

• Cold-water fish	Salmon, mackerel, tuna, sablefish, herring, anchovies, sardines, rainbow trout, Alaska king and blue crab, oysters, bass, catfish, halibut, cod, shrimp, pilchard, flounder, haddock, and bluefish.
• Fresh-water fish	Trout and crappie.
• Fiber	Oats, apples, peas, prunes, and legumes such as black-eyed peas, all beans such as kidney, pinto, and navy, and agar-agar seaweed gelatin.
• Vegetables, fruits, and whole grains	All varieties, especially antioxidant-rich leafy greens, deep yellow vegetables; cruciferous family of broccoli, cabbage, brussels sprouts, cauliflower, and turnips rich in indoles or cancer inhibitors.
• Water	Eight glasses a day keeps fat washed away.
• Supplements	GLA, EPA; the support vitamins niacin (B-3), B-6, C, and E; antioxidant beta carotene; the minerals zinc, magnesium, and selenium.
• Aerobic exercise	30-minute walk at vigorous pace outside in sunlight or equivalent aerobic activity like dancing, swimming, or bicycling.

Prime Offenders

These foods are most affected by heat, oxidation, hydrogenation, or homogenization and should be avoided.

- Trans or damaged fats

  Margarine, shortening, and baked goods containing hydrogenated oils such as breads, cookies, cakes, and taco shells; commercial vegetable oils; commercial peanut butter; all fried foods.

- Homogenized fats

  Full-fat and low-fat (2 percent) homogenized cow's milk and dairy product derivatives such as cheese and yogurt.

- Oxidized cholesterol

  Dried milk, dried eggs, dried custard mixes, smoked fish, aged cheese.

These foods biochemically sabotage the metabolism.

- White refined sugar

  Cakes, cookies, candies, pies, and soft drinks. Eliminate and eat only natural sources from fresh fruit.

- Alcohol

  Use only in cooking (the alcohol burns off and the flavor remains).

- Saturated fats

  All animal fats, particularly beef tallow, and palm oil (used in most fast food preparation); coconut oil (used in nondairy creamers) and palm oil both found in shortening, some soups, whipped topping, some frostings, frozen entrees, cookies, and snack foods. Palm kernel oil is an ingredient in carob candies.

Nutritional Bombshells

As you now know from the preceding chapters, it isn't the fat itself that is a problem, but what we do *to* the fat. When I first discovered this, I began to explore every facet of food, from selection to handling to storage to cooking methods, and food combinations and cooking utensils. I uncovered some surprising nutritional insights that discredit many accepted nutritional truths. Now we know:

- A high-carbohydrate diet emphasizing a high grain intake may be energy-draining and harmful to a growing number of people.
- Cooking with polyunsaturated oils is more dangerous than using small amounts of saturated fat, such as butter.
- Homogenized milk may be the real underlying cause of heart disease, not cholesterol.
- Cholesterol-free margarines can be devastating to health.
- Exercising in daylight is distinctly more beneficial than exercising indoors.

But there is more surprising information that is covered in chapter 13, "The New Nutrition Diet Master Strategy." There you will discover:

- If you cook with aluminum, what you're cooking in may have as much influence over your health as what you are cooking.
- Frozen fruits and vegetables can be more nutritious than their fresh counterparts.
- Rare is rarely the most healthy way to cook fish or meat.
- Red meats have a very important place in a well-balanced diet.

The Life in Your Food

Cooking is actually a form of chemistry. It can either protect or destroy food value and nutrients. Canning, freezing, storage, and cooking all create vitamin and mineral loss that can affect good health.

In canning, for example, there can be a 40 to 60 percent loss of vitamins. While freezing retains more vitamins, there still may be up to a 45 percent loss in the blanching process necessary to neutralize enzymes.

From the time of harvesting to shipping, warehouse storage of lettuce, spinach, and potatoes can result in a loss of up to 50 percent of their vitamin C. Because of the time elapsed from harvesting to the supermarket shelf, fresh produce can be less nutritious in certain cases than even the frozen variety. Furthermore, if the fresh produce is stored at too high a temperature in shipping or storage, additional loss of thiamin (vitamin B-1), riboflavin (vitamin B-2), niacin (vitamin B-3), and vitamin C can result. Fresh produce always should be stored on ice or in an area cooler than room temperature.

Cooking with too much water depletes vitamins B and C, while using baking soda to keep vegetables green is another potent destroyer of vitamin C.

Food Follies

The way in which food is cooked and handled can mean the difference between health and disease. Frying and prolonged broiling of meat and fish produce genetic changes in bacteria known to cause cancer in test animals. Food-poisoning bacteria like salmonella are found in raw meats, eggs, poultry, fish, shellfish, and milk. These foods may taste just fine but still be infected. All cutting boards, knives, and plates used in the preparation of raw meat and poultry must be thoroughly washed before reusing them for cooked food. Pathogenic organisms can be transferred from infected food to cooked foods to you. The result can be those flulike symptoms that last a few hours to a few days, now so common that people don't even consult a doctor when they occur. Even worse, food poisoning can cause chronic joint problems such as arthritis and other rheumatoid diseases, according to the FDA's Dr. Douglas Archer, director of the Microbiology division.

The FDA believes that in 1985 about 4 million Americans were infected with salmonella: 35,000 were hospitalized. But who knows how many people actually had salmonella in their dinner and never knew what hit them? The USDA estimates that 30 percent of all poultry in this country is salmonella-infected due to the processing of chicken. Some researchers suggest that the number is actually much closer to 60 percent.

I have designed the New Nutrition Diet Master Menu Plan for good eating and healthful food preparation. All foods you will be eating are considered. You will learn the best ways to select, prepare, serve, and store them. Remember, your kitchen is your personal laboratory. Observing simple rules of chemistry in food preparation can mean a great health savings not only in terms of greater nutritional value, but in the avoidance of routine illnesses that start in the kitchen.

Nutritional Savvy

The first rule is that heat, light, soaking in water, and extended exposure to air can destroy valuable vitamins as well as the beneficial fats. High temperatures and oxidation can alter fatty acid bonds and create rancidity. Amino acids (the building blocks of protein) become unusable by the body when protein foods are overheated, as in frying. An innocent-looking piece of fried chicken, for example, has not only whopping numbers of extra calories, but its protein is less valuable.

Vegetables cut long before they're used, salad-bar style, have lost many nutrients.

The B vitamins are especially vulnerable to heat and light. Riboflavin (vitamin B-2) is the most sensitive to light, which is why many dairies now use cardboard cartons instead of glass bottles to contain milk, a good source of riboflavin. (Deficiency symptoms include cracks around the corners of the mouth and eyes, eye burning, pupil dilation, oily skin, and fatigue.)

Both vitamins B and C are water-soluble and easily lost from produce soaked longer than one hour. The lesson in all of this:

1. Low, slow cooking.
2. The less water touches the food, the better for vitamins.
3. Prepare food right before you cook it.

Temperature Control

Exposure to room-temperature air can oxidize the cholesterol in animal foods, causing altered blood chemistry. No animal food, such as meat, fish, cheese, milk, eggs, or butter, should be left standing outside the refrigerator for more than two hours.

A simple rule always to keep in mind is: Keep hot foods hot (140 degrees and above) and cold foods cold (40 degrees and lower). See the chart on temperature of food for control of bacteria.

Most of us take our refrigerators for granted. Understanding how this appliance can help you in properly caring for food is a cornerstone for good nutrition.

1. Adjust your refrigerator temperature to 40 degrees.
2. The freezer should be kept at zero degrees.
3. Get a thermometer if your freezer indicates only HIGH or LOW temperature levels.
4. Check frost levels. If more than one-quarter inch of frost builds up, the cooling process is slowed down. It is time to defrost.

Temperature of Food For Control of Bacteria

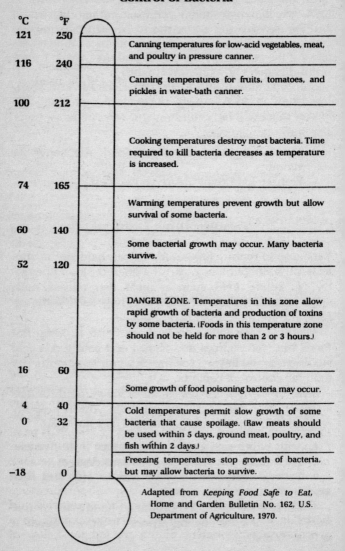

°C	°F	
121	250	Canning temperatures for low-acid vegetables, meat, and poultry in pressure canner.
116	240	
		Canning temperatures for fruits, tomatoes, and pickles in water-bath canner.
100	212	
		Cooking temperatures destroy most bacteria. Time required to kill bacteria decreases as temperature is increased.
74	165	
		Warming temperatures prevent growth but allow survival of some bacteria.
60	140	
		Some bacterial growth may occur. Many bacteria survive.
52	120	
		DANGER ZONE. Temperatures in this zone allow rapid growth of bacteria and production of toxins by some bacteria. (Foods in this temperature zone should not be held for more than 2 or 3 hours.)
16	60	
		Some growth of food poisoning bacteria may occur.
4	40	Cold temperatures permit slow growth of some bacteria that cause spoilage. (Raw meats should be used within 5 days, ground meat, poultry, and fish within 2 days.)
0	32	
		Freezing temperatures stop growth of bacteria, but may allow bacteria to survive.
−18	0	

Adapted from *Keeping Food Safe to Eat*, Home and Garden Bulletin No. 162, U.S. Department of Agriculture, 1970.

Other Helpful Hints

• Do not stack foods on top of one another in the refrigerator. Circulation of cold air is important to prevent spoilage.

• Store perishables where you can see them. Fish gravies and meat broths should be used up in two days.

The following indicators on the oven or stove translate into temperatures:

- Warm   = 125 to 200 degrees
- Boiling = 212 to 300 degrees
- Frying = 350 degrees and above

When food is kept over a long period of time, it should be held in the oven at 140 degrees or higher to prevent bacteria from growing. Get a meat thermometer to accurately measure the temperature of food.

Selection of Vegetables and Fruits

Follow these guidelines to get the most nutritional mileage from your food:

Select fresh vegetables, preferably locally grown. This is a first step to ensure that nutrients have not been lost during shipping and storing. Frozen is the next-best choice. Many vegetables and fruits are frozen at the peak of ripeness in their growing season, so taste can be exceptionally flavorful in certain vegetables such as peas, corn, and lima beans. Just remember that if your vegetables are frozen (and this goes for frozen food in general, by the way), thaw them in the refrigerator and then cook them immediately to prevent bacteria from spreading.

Hydroponic (soilless) growing of fruits, vegetables, and herbs is a promising agricultural development. In a greenhouse environment plants are fed by a flow of water rich in essential nutrients. Growth is enhanced, and the food produced is often much higher in vitamins and minerals than that of soil-fed plants. Yet, the long-term effects of consumption by humans has not been assessed—there may be other essential factors from the soil that cannot be duplicated in a soilless environment. These effects are electromagnetic and cannot be measured by conventional science, so the verdict is not yet in.

Remember that moldy, soggy, or discolored patches on celery, broccoli, or cauliflower are a sign of deterioration. Root vegetables with wilted or watery leaves should be avoided. Do not buy potatoes that are green or sprouting. This indicates the presence of a toxin called solanine. Carrots with hairy roots are also nutrient-deprived.

Remember that fully matured vegetables have the most nutrition of all. Sweet red peppers, for example, have 7.5 times more vitamin A than immature green peppers. Ripe red tomatoes contain 3.5 times more vitamin A than green tomatoes.

Certain varieties of produce give you better nutrition for your money. Romaine lettuce, for example, has more than twice the iron, calcium, and vitamin C of iceberg.

Successful Vegetable Storage

• Do not store vegetables with fruits. The natural gas that fruits produce when ripening—ethylene— can make vegetables deteriorate.

• Store vegetables in lower bins away from the freezer section to prevent crystallization. Store dry and wash right before use, unless you are using a Clorox bath to cleanse all produce before storing (see p. 129). Excess moisture encourages mold growth.

• Store greens leafy side down in a twist-tied plastic bag. Before closing the bag, retain a little air inside to keep the greens from wilting.

• Store root vegetables such as potatoes, onions, hard-skinned squash, and yams in a cool,
dry pantry (50–70 degrees) away from direct
sunlight.

Like vegetables, certain fruits are better health buys.
Pink grapefruit are 50 times higher in vitamin A than
white grapefruit. Oranges from California are 34 percent
higher in vitamin C than Florida oranges. Avocados
grown in California are 15 percent higher in fat, which
may account for their superior flavor, than those from
Florida.

Many frozen fruits are actually a better buy than the
fresh variety. Frozen berries—blueberries, raspberries,
strawberries, blackberries, and boysenberries—are generally uniformly sweet and flavorful. Fresh berries, by
the time they reach the market, are often overripe and
spoiled from handling. Those at the bottom of the bas-
ket are sometimes crushed and inedible. Mold forms
almost instantly on a crushed berry.

Successful Fruit Storage

Store fruits dry and wash right before eating. Unripened
fruits such as melons, bananas, avocados, peaches, plums,
pears, and tomatoes can be kept in a dry, cool pantry
away from direct sunlight. Lemons, limes, grapefruit,
and oranges can be kept in the pantry, too. Fully ripened fruit should be kept in the refrigerator bins. Berries should be stored covered.

Vegetable Preparation and Cooking

Limit cutting, peeling, and soaking of vegetables. Exposure to air, light, and water robs essential vitamins and
minerals. Cook over low heat and keep the lid on during cooking.

Vegetables can be prepared by cooking in a covered

pan, Crockpot, or stainless steel steamer. They also can be prepared by poaching or sautéing, in a very small amount of virgin olive oil, canola oil, peanut oil, or butter. Other vegetable oils produce dangerous free radicals when heated, so use the more stable olive or peanut oil or butter (one tablespoon) for cooking.

Never bake vegetables uncovered unless you are using a microwave oven. Dry heat evaporates natural juices, where most of the vitamins and minerals are contained. When baking vegetables (and this goes for baked potatoes, especially), bake in a covered container at 350 degrees or below. To obtain the crispy skin of baked potatoes, uncover for the last ten to fifteen minutes of cooking.

Fruit Preparation and Cooking

Ultimately, it is more important that fruit be fully ripened than whether it is fresh, frozen, or canned in its own juices. Frozen and canned fruit in its own juice are harvested at the peak of ripeness and so are good fruit choices. Unripened fruit creates gas, bloating, and much digestive discomfort.

Fruit fibers are more easily broken down in cooking than are vegetable fibers. Fruit sugar therefore becomes more concentrated in the bloodstream without the fiber to regulate its release. This is why raw, ripe fruit is more desirable than cooked fruit for those who want to control their blood sugar levels.

There are two fruits, however, in which the health value is actually enhanced by cooking. These are blueberries and blackberries. These fruits, in their raw state, contain a thiamin-destroying enzyme. Thiamin (vitamin B-1) is essential for the nervous system and is known as the "morale vitamin." When the berries are cooked (or frozen), the enzyme is deactivated.

"Baked" rather than "raw" apples are better tolerated by people who have digestive problems.

Fish, Fowl and Meat

Whether purchased fresh (which is preferred) or frozen, all flesh foods must be cooked. If frozen, they should be thawed in the refrigerator and then cooked immediately after defrosting. Both fowl and meat thaw at the rate of one pound per hour. Again, all utensils as well as hands that come in contact with raw fish, fowl, and meat must be thoroughly washed to prevent bacterial infection.

Cooking temperatures must reach 160 to 180 degrees to kill disease-causing bacteria and other organisms. Most such organisms are destroyed at 140 degrees, but to ensure that all parts of the food are thoroughly heated, cooking at 160 to 180 degrees guarantees a safety margin against the heartier "bugs."

Undercooked, rare, or raw flesh foods can carry the eggs of such parasites as tapeworm (in fish and beef), liver flukes (beef), and the parasites that cause toxoplasmosis (beef and lamb). These organisms can seriously and chronically affect nutrient absorption and overall health. Parasitic disease is hard to trace, so symptoms such as cramps, diarrhea, constipation, and muscular aches and pains can go on for years.

Raw flesh foods such as sushi (raw fish), steak tartare, and carpaccio (raw beef) are definitely *not* recommended. Fish should be cooked so that all parts flake easily. Beef should be cooked to medium (160 degrees), and poultry should contain no pink areas and the joints should be easily movable.

Successful Meat Storage

• Refrigerate or freeze all raw meat, fish, and poultry immediately to prevent bacteria growth.

• When you refrigerate, choose the coldest section nearest the freezer, and cook as soon as possible.

• An uncooked chicken can remain only up to two days before spoilage sets in. Cooked chicken lasts up to five days.

• Cooked meats last longer when stored with sauces or gravies containing vegetables such as onions, peppers, potatoes, and tomatoes, which are high in the antioxidant vitamins A, E, and C. The fat in the meat can combine with oxygen in the refrigerator, allowing rancidity to set in. The vegetables protect the meat.

Help Line

The U.S. Department of Agriculture operates a Meat and Poultry Hotline at (800) 535-4555 between 10:00 A.M. and 4:00 P.M., Monday through Friday. Experts can answer everything you ever wanted to know about handling meat and fowl.

Shellfish

Like other fish, all shellfish should be cooked. Uncooked shellfish such as clams and oysters carry hepatitis A and Norwalk virus. These viruses can easily be mistaken for the flu because their symptoms are similar. Raw shellfish from contaminated waters offer more serious— and sometimes deadly—problems. Furthermore, there is an enzyme present in raw clams and oysters that destroys thiamin (vitamin B-1). Steam clams for an optimum of six minutes.

Seeds, Peanuts, Nuts, Beans, Egg Whites and Potatoes

Although these seemingly random foods don't appear to have much in common, they do in one respect: they all should be cooked for maximum health benefits. This group contains enzyme inhibitors that interfere with proper digestion, creating gas, heartburn, and gastrointestinal problems. The enzyme inhibitors are destroyed by cooking. In the case of seeds, nuts, and beans, the enzyme inhibitors can also be deactivated by sprouting. First soak for six hours, then sprout. Toasting is another way to deactivate the inhibitors. All seeds and nuts, and peanuts (technically a legume) can be "home toasted" in the oven (see p. 108).

Always cook your eggs and potatoes. Raw egg whites contain avidin, a protein that inhibits biotin (a vitamin of the vitamin B complex family) absorption. When you cook eggs for thirty seconds or more, the avidin is destroyed, thus allowing full release of biotin for the body.

Many people soak grains before eating. Soaking increases digestibility of wheat, rye, oats, and barley (the higher-gluten grains) without digestive upsets. Simply soak in water overnight and cook the next morning.

Desirable Cooking Methods

Stir sautéing	Cooking in small amounts of liquid or oil (water, peanut oil, canola oil, virgin olive oil, vegetable broth, or defatted chicken broth) at medium heat. Do not use polyunsaturated vegetable oils such as safflower or corn, which are extremely heat sensitive.
Steaming	Cooking over boiling water in a large or small steamer pot, stainless steel folding basket, or Chinese-style tiered bamboo steamer. Steaming preserves nutrients, color, and texture, and accentuates flavor while keeping in moisture. The leftover liquid can be used for soups or stir sautéing.

When cooking highly concentrated carbohydrate foods such as sweet potatoes and yams, steam instead of baking. The baking temperatures precipitate the natural sugar into a caramelized substance, changing the complex carbohydrate into a simple sugar.

Broiling

Cooking in a broiler with overhead direct heat. Keep the oven door open. Nutrients are destroyed when the oven door is closed because the food dehydrates when surrounded by dry heat.

Toasting

Cooking in the oven at baking temperatures below 300 degrees. Seeds and nuts should be "home toasted." Low-level heating deactivates the enzyme inhibitors. Heating above 300 degrees, common in commercial roasting practices, changes the oil from the natural cis form to the damaged trans form.

Baking

Cooking in covered utensils with minimum liquid to retain moistness.

Microwave

Microwave cooking heats the food by friction of the food's molecules. This is opposite to other cooking methods, in which the outside air surrounding the food must first be heated before the food begins to cook. Cooking in a microwave does not make the food radioactive despite the common misconception. Microwave cooking may even protect vitamins and minerals better than conventional methods but care must be taken with certain foods. Because microwaves do not cook uniformly, rotating meats such as chicken and pork is necessary to protect against salmonella in the chicken and trichina in the pork.

Food prepared in a microwave may not be as visually appealing or appetizing because it does not brown after cooking. Convection microwave ovens or ovens with special browning features can achieve a more finished food look.

Undesirable Cooking Methods

Avoid frying

Frying is an all too common technique used in coffeeshops and restaurants, as well as in the preparation of popular snack foods such as doughnuts, potato chips, and many bakery products. Tasty as these foods are, overheating of polyunsaturated oils produces more free radicals than overheating of saturated fats. These foods should carry the Surgeon General's warning. Frying meat, fish, or chicken also makes the protein bond indigestible.

When palm or coconut oil is used for frying, there are many less free radicals formed because these oils are saturated. Too much of the saturated oils present another problem, though, because their presence can block the natural cis linoleic from transforming to the vital GLA. Plus, harmful toxins that have been associated with cancer are produced no matter what source of fat is used when heated at high temperatures (350 degrees) or reheated with the same oil source. When you do fry, do not reheat the oil; throw it out.

Avoid browning or charring or

The oxidative reaction of charcoal grilling (a combination of browning and charring) is toxic and can be carcino-

| charcoal grilling | genic. Further, food soaks up added chemicals from the charcoal briquettes. One piece of barbecued meat may be the carcinogenic equivalent of sixty cigarettes. It would be wise to cut off any burned, charred, or blackened portions of meat. Charcoal broiling should be avoided. |

Gas grilling—with adequate ventilation —is acceptable if there is no sensitivity to hydrocarbons, the toxic byproducts of gas combustion.

| Avoid pressure cooking | The temperatures are too high and destroy vitamins. This method is suitable, however, for canning foods at home. |

| More fuel for thought | It is better to use electric rather than gas ranges and ovens for your cooking needs. The pilot lights and burners on gas ranges can release low levels of carbon monoxide and nitrous dioxide that often go undetected because they are invisible and odorless. Undiagnosable psychiatric conditions have even been traced to natural gas leakages. Symptoms such as dizziness, headache, confusion, chronic fatigue, insomnia, and respiratory problems can have their roots in unrecognized gas emissions. If you suspect that you may be suffering from "indoor pollution," have your local gas company come to your house and check for a gas leak. |

Essential Utensils

| • Stainless steel | Heavy stainless steel waterless cookware cooks food in a vacuum seal in its own juices. This is more expensive than the |

regular stainless, which is also desirable, but can protect mineral and vitamin content more thoroughly.

- Enamel
- Corning Ware
- Glass   Purists beware. Because glass and Pyrex do let in light, they may allow small amounts of light-sensitive riboflavin to become depleted.

- Pyrex
- Iron   The extra iron picked up from cooking is good for you. When spaghetti sauce, for example, is cooked in iron pots, it contains six times more iron than when made in ceramic cookware.

Baking equipment should be heavy-duty tin or black steel. Glass, stainless steel bowls, cling-free plastic wrap, or plastic bags (the kind used in the produce section of the supermarket) are best for food storage and freezing. There is also a hypoallergenic cellophane bag now available at health food stores for more sensitive individuals. The above mentioned materials do not dissolve into the food.

I have discovered a marvelous mini food slicer called the Zyliss, which has three grating attachments. There are several advantages to this simple all-purpose cutter. It is easy to assemble, easy to clean, portable for traveling, and needs no electrical attachment. Best of all, the price is only fifteen dollars.

Essential Utensil Alert

It may seem as though we live in an ultracivilized, totally sanitary environment, but in fact there are some potentially dangerous situations common to almost every American kitchen. They're all easy to remedy, so give some thought to the following.

- *Throw out all cracked dishes.*

Bacteria can live in the cracks of cups and plates. These bacteria will mix with hot beverages or foods, creating digestive problems.

- *Replace or Clorox wooden cutting and chopping boards.*

Again, bacteria can live in the cracks of wooden blocks. Use a Lucite chopping board, or give your wooden board a Clorox rinse (use approximately ten drops of Clorox to a quart of water).

- *Avoid unlined copper pots and pans.*

Copper can contaminate acidic food and destroy vitamin C, and is antagonistic to zinc. Brass containers usually contain copper, so do not store food in them.

- *Eliminate aluminum and aluminum foil.*

No food or drink, especially acidic foods that are tomato based, should be cooked or covered in aluminum or aluminum foil.

Aluminum can affect digestion by destroying the protein-digestive enzyme pepsin in the stomach. It also hampers the body's utilization of calcium, magnesium, and phosphorus as well as vitamin A. Impaired memory and motor coordination as well as Alzheimer's disease and osteoporosis have been linked to systemic aluminum toxicity. The kidneys, brain, and gastrointestinal tract are the target areas where aluminum accumulates and can cause problems.

This metal is also found in antacids such as Maalox, Mylanta, Gelusil, Di-Gel, and Rolaids. Studies have shown that even small amounts of antacids can inhibit intestinal absorption of fluoride and phosphorus, causing increased elimination of calcium. Since calcium loss is a prime factor in osteoporosis—the bone-thinning disease— the answer is not more calcium but less aluminum.

Pain relievers such as Arthritis-Strength Bufferin, Ascriptin, Bufferin, Pabirin, and Vanquish contain aluminum.

• *Parchment paper: the foil to aluminum foil.*

Instead of aluminum foil for cooking and reheating, use parchment paper. It is available in most health food stores and is excellent for retaining flavor because the food cooks in its own juice. Made from wood pulp, it is a healthy alternative to metals and plastics. Ideal for vegetables and fish (as New Orleans cooks have known for years), parchment paper can be used for baking and poaching. The food is placed on top of a moistened parchment sheet, then the corners are gathered up and tied securely.

• *Aluminum-proof the kitchen.*

Check all steamers, measuring cups, spoons, bread pans, and cookie sheets. These items can all be safely replaced by Pyrex, stainless steel, or dairy tin (an old-fashioned baking material).

It may also be a good idea to replace aluminum-containing baking powders, as well as deodorants and antiperspirants, to generally reduce exposure to aluminum buildup, which accumulates in the body and can progressively deposit in the organs, muscles, and tissues. Aluminum, because of its astringent quality, irritates mucous membranes in the gastrointestinal tract.

• *The great outdoors.*

When camping out, remember to take extra care with certain foods. Ground meat is more subject to oxidation than whole meat. Cook it as soon as possible.

Do not drink water from streams and lakes, because many are contaminated with a protozoa called *Giardia lamblia*. This amoebalike one-celled animal can cause chronic diarrhea. It makes its home in the upper gastrointestinal tract and gallbladder.

Boil all questionable water for at least ten minutes at a rolling boil.

13

THE NEW
NUTRITION DIET
MASTER STRATEGY

*Now learn what and how great benefits a
temperate diet will bring with it.*
—HORACE

When you buy foods that are as near to nature as
possible, you need not be concerned about deciphering
food labels. It is only when foods are jarred, packaged,
dehydrated, frozen, canned, pouched, or otherwise processed that we need to become alert to extra fat, salt,
and sugar—not to mention over three thousand additives in the form of chemical preservatives, colorings,
and flavorings.

A little primer will help to remedy the situation. There
is a label pecking order that is easy to remember when
doing your detective work on decoding. The first ingredient is the one found in the greatest quantity in the
product, while the ingredient listed last is the one found
in the least amount. Try to make sure that any questionable
ingredient (such as processed fat, salt, sugar, additives,
or colorings) comes after the third item on the list.

Finding Fat

Fat, no matter what the label may read, is still considered fat and usually undesirable fat. Key words that can

translate into trans, damaged, or excessive saturated fat include margarine, shortening, vegetable oil, mayonnaise, lard, suet, tallow, and mono-, di-, and triglycerides. Mineral oil is a nonnutritive substance that can flush fat-soluble vitamins out of the system, and should be avoided. A label that reads "100% vegetable oil" may not only be a heat-treated and therefore damaged oil, but it can be the cover for palm kernel or coconut oil—the most saturated oils of all.

Some oils that are not derived from food crops, such as cottonseed oil, are not subject to FDA regulations for pesticide safety. Cottonseed oil is often an ingredient in margarine— another reason to avoid it.

Shaking Salt

Watch for added sodium in the form of sodium combinations, brine, baking soda, and especially MSG (monosodium glutamate). Foods containing soy sauce or tamari should be shunned, as soy sauce packs a walloping 1,000 mg. of sodium per tablespoon. This is too much sodium at one time when many must limit their total sodium intake to a maximum of 2,000 mg. per day. The salt-reduced varieties may also be excessive when you consider that the same tablespoon contains 500 mg. of sodium and you tend to use twice as much to attain the same flavor.

The Yeast Problem: The Twentieth Century Epidemic

Many of my patients who eliminate soy sauce from their foods lose pounds of stored water weight. This fermented, wheat-containing product also contributes to yeast overgrowth and adds to systemic candidiasis—an increasing problem because of too much sugar, birth control pills, steroids, drugs, and unmonitored use of antibiotics.

Candida albicans has been aptly named the Twentieth Century Disease. Normally not a problem in a healthy body, the yeast overgrows in the intestines when the immune system is depressed. Antibiotics, whether taken directly for medical reasons or ingested indirectly through antibiotic-fed livestock, kill the beneficial intestinal microflora bacteria that normally control the *Candida*.

It is interesting to note that a *Candida*-control diet restricts sugar and high-carbohydrate foods, particularly those made from gluten-containing grains. Fruits and yeast-related foods such as mushrooms, cheeses, tomato sauces, soy sauce, and vinegar are also restricted or eliminated. All of these *Candida* considerations are built into the Master Menu Plan and dietary recommendations.

Sweet Surrender

With regard to hidden sugar, watch out for words ending in "ose," such as sucrose, dextrose, and lactose. Corn syrup and fructose (which is usually derived from corn) may seem fairly natural, but are actually adding to your total sugar intake and can insidiously contribute to elevated triglyceride levels.

Where to Shop

Most of the staples for the New Nutrition Diet can be purchased at your local supermarket or fruit and vegetable stand.* Extra virgin olive oil, for example, can be

---

*Many of my patients clean their food in a special detoxifying bath that removes sprays, bacteria, fungus, parasites, and heavy metals. The formula is included on p. 129. For those who prefer to buy food from suppliers of organic foods who do not use animal drugs, pesticides, and sprays, see p. 130 for a list of organic food mail-order suppliers. This list is provided by the Center for Science in the Public Interest's Americans for Safe Food Project based in Washington, D.C.

located in the specialty or gourmet section of the super-market. Other New Nutrition oils and nuts and seeds will more likely be found at your health food store, where whole grains, flours, thickeners, bulk grains, and cereals may also be located.

When shopping at your health food store, a word of caution is in order. The terms *natural* and *pure* have no real meaning in food advertising. You may think that there is a preselection of only "health" foods when in a natural foods store. However, most of the highly touted natural granola cereals, the pure and natural candy bars, and vegetarian frozen entrees usually contain as much fat as their supermarket equivalents. Nearly half the calories of a popular health food line of frozen entrees come from fat. And this company advertises its fare as "light and lean."

Health food stores stock high-fat products in the form of nut butters, raw-milk cheeses, full-fat yogurts, and kefir. Salt adds up quickly in tamari, tempeh, and tex-tured vegetable protein, while sugar masquerades in the form of blackstrap molasses, pure turbinado sugar, honey, rice syrup, and barley malt.

Before You Take a Bite

It has been said that it is not just the food that counts but what your body does with it. How true this is when you understand that we derive *no* value from foods that are not digested. Even Mark Twain knew that the aver-age person "eats too much and chews too little!" Proper chewing to assure good digestion is of paramount im-portance. Although the main focus of the rest of this book is the 21-Day Master Menu Plan, which includes recipes, keep this nutritional fact in mind: this program will do you little good if your body can't absorb the nutrients you have so conscientiously prepared.

So, here is a most helpful hint to enhance digestion:

- Chew your food thoroughly—at least thirty times per bite, please.

Remember that ptyalin, the starch-digesting enzyme in saliva, is located in the mouth. The more you chew, the better your stomach and GI tract will behave.

Food Combinations

I have noticed over the years that with many patients, digestion and assimilation have improved when foods are combined in certain ways. Intestinal discomfort such as gas, bloating, diarrhea, and constipation, as well as food allergies, may relate to incompatible food combinations. These observations have been built into the New Nutrition Diet plan but bear repeating for personal menu planning and nutritional guidance. Try them out on yourself; your stomach may thank you forever. I also have found that as long as proper food combining is followed, counting calories becomes unnecessary.

These combinations appear to assist digestion:

- Protein and green vegetables. If you want to add starch, use rice, potato, millet, or corn. (Example: baked fish, green leafy salad, and brown rice.)

- Starch and vegetables. (Example: baked potato and steamed broccoli with carrots.)

- Melons and citrus fruits eaten alone.

- Eggs seem to be neutral and can be enjoyed in most combinations. They complement beans, vegetables, and dairy products. They go well with the grain starches. (Example: omelets, quiche, and toast and eggs.)

These combinations encourage digestive upsets:

- Flesh protein (fish, fowl, and beef) and gluten-rich grain starches (wheat, rye, oats, and barley). (Example: fillet of fish sandwich on a whole wheat bun.) The bran component from wheat and oats, however, does not contain gluten and can be used with flesh proteins.

• Vegetables and fruit eaten together. Save your fruit dessert for at least two hours after a vegetable meal. The exceptions to this rule are enzyme-rich papaya and pineapple, which are natural digestive aids and can be eaten with most foods.

• Milk and meat. (Example: a glass of milk with a roast beef dinner.)

• Water taken with meals before food is swallowed. While water is necessary for digestion, the saliva activity is weakened when water is used to wash down food. Extremely hot or cold water depresses gastric juices and acts as a shock to the system.

Stocking and Storing the Staples

Listed below are some basic foods with storage information that fit the criteria for New Nutrition living. Brand names are used when generic product descriptions are not specific enough to assure high food quality and nutritive value suitable for the New Nutrition Diet. For your convenience, several recommended brands are shown in parentheses but are not necessarily the only brands that meet quality standards.

The basic rule of thumb is to *buy right, then keep away from heat, air, and light!*

Oils   Unrefined safflower, sunflower, sesame, soy, corn, peanut, linseed, walnut, almond, hazelnut, canola (Arrowhead Mills, Erewhon, Norganic, Westbrae, Walnut Acres, Eden, Jaffee

Brothers, Spectrum). Extra virgin and virgin olive oil (Siabica, Walnut Acres, Golden Eagle, Old Monk, Westbrae, Jaffee Brothers).

Most imported virgin oils from Spain, Greece, and Italy are acceptable. Remember that unprocessed oils contain sediment, are somewhat cloudy, and have a stronger taste, all signs of unrefined quality. The color of natural unrefined oils is related to the original source: olive oil is green, safflower oil is yellow, corn oil is orange, and soy oil is dark brown.

Storage Tips:
Refrigerate most oils in tightly capped bottles. Tinted glass or tin is the best storage protector. Olive oil can be kept in a cool, dark place. Buy crude oil in small amounts and use it up within a short time after opening. Exposure to air and light can create rancidity.

Nuts and Seeds

Raw, unshelled almonds, filberts, pecans, walnuts; pumpkin, sunflower, poppy, caraway, flaxseed. Sesame seeds and sesame butter.

When selecting sesame seeds, choose a company that uses a mechanical hulling method rather than chemicals to dehull the seeds (International Protein Industries, Protein Aide, Arrowhead Mills, Westbrae). Nut butters other than sesame seed butter are not recommended because they can become rancid so easily. The oil in sesame seeds has great durability against rancidity.

Storage Tips:
Store nuts and seeds in the shell in the natural, unroasted state in a cool dry place. The refrigerator or freezer are good environments for nuts. Flaxseed especially must be ground right before cooking to avoid rancidity. Never use the whole flaxseed.

Mayonnaise

(Walnut Acres, Hain, Hollywood, Westbrae.)

Dairy

Nonfat milk, yogurt (Dannon and Continental nonfat yogurt), and cottage cheese; sweet butter; grated Parmesan cheese occasionally; goat cheese, feta cheese, goat yogurt.

Dairy substitutes: fresh or powdered soymilk (Jolly Joan, Fearn, Energy Foods); tofu.

Storage Tips:
Keep milk and all milk products nearest the freezer section. Do not leave out more than two hours or cholesterol will oxidize.

Eggs: Fresh have the best flavor; use within one week of purchase.

Storage Tips:
To store separated eggs, pour cold water over the yolk and refrigerate up to four days. The egg white just needs to be covered with water.

Protein

Fish: All, especially the Omega-3 types such as salmon, mackerel, sardines, tuna, herring, trout, cod, flounder, butterfish, pilchard. Canned salmon, tuna, anchovies, mackerel. If packed in oil or salt, drain well under running water (Featherweight, Seasons, Lillie, Three Star).

Seafood: Shrimp, lobster, crab, scallops, calamari.

Poultry: White meat of skinned turkey and skinned chicken. Nitrate-free, uncured cooked turkey and chicken sausage (Health Valley, Harmony Farms).

Beef: Good or standard grades; flank, rump, round, chuck.

Lamb: Leg, loin, rib (avoid fatty shank and breast).

Veal: Shoulder, rib, loin (avoid fatty breast).

Tofu: In amounts comparable to fish, poultry, or lean meat.

Vegetables

All fresh in-season produce, when available. If fresh is not available, frozen is next best, followed by canned or jarred with no added salt. Water chestnuts, bamboo shoots, and artichoke hearts are readily available canned. Jarred fire-roasted red peppers are also on market shelves. Daikon radish, sunchokes (Jerusalem artichokes), and sprouted mixed beans make great nibbles and exotic salad additions. Low-sodium V-8 juice is good to keep on hand. See Vegetables listed on p. 203 under Food Equivalents for complete variety.

Fruits

Fresh, seasonally ripe, locally grown fruits are first choice when available and without mold. The next choice is frozen, and last is canned in natural unsweetened juices. See Fruits listed on p. 204 under Food Equivalents for complete variety.

Unsweetened fruit preserves, applebutter, and cranberry sauce conserve are also acceptable (Westbrae, Pure & Simple, Walnut Acres, Sorrell Ridge).

Fruit juices: Unsweetened apple, cherry, pineapple-coconut, pomegranate, papaya, cranberry, or cranberry sweetened with grape concentrate (Hansen, L&A, Walnut Acres, Shoosh, Wagners).

Grains	Unrefined whole grains such as whole pearl barley, bulgar, brown rice, buckwheat groats (kasha), corn meal, millet, steel-cut oats, rye, triticale, wild rice, whole wheat (Arrowhead Mills, Erewhon).
	Storage Tips: Store in air-tight containers for up to one month and then refrigerate. During the summer months, store in refrigerator after one week.
Cereals	Sugar-free, low-salt, no-preservative cereals hot and cold such as Wheatena, cream of rye, oat bran, cream of rice, 4- and 7-grain; barley flakes, oat flakes, corn flakes, soy grits, puffed wheat, puffed oats, puffed rye, puffed millet, NutriGrain, shredded wheat, Grapenuts, Spicer's NutriWheat. (Quaker, Kellogg's, Arrowhead Mills, Hadley's, Pure & Simple, Health Valley, New Morning, Erewhon).
Crackers	Scandinavian-style crisp breads, fiber crisps, rice snaps, rice tea cakes, rye crackers, whole wheat wafers, whole wheat matzo (Kavli, WasaBrod, AkMak, Fantastik Foods, Pacific Rice Products, Manischewitz).

Breads	Whole grain, free of chemicals and hydrogenated fats and processed oils. Pita, Pritikin whole wheat, rye, English muffins, sprouted grain, Essene bread (Ezekial 4:9, Health Valley, Life Stream, Food For Life). Rice cakes and corn tortillas.
	Storage Tips: Refrigerate or freeze to protect natural fats from becoming rancid with exposure to room-temperature air.
Pasta	Whole-wheat spaghetti, noodles, shells, and macaroni, corn pasta, cellophane rice and mung bean noodles, soba (buckwheat noodles). (Health Valley, de Boles, Maikun, Erewhon). Lupini pasta with 60% less gluten and four times more fiber than ordinary pasta is now available from IN-AG.
Flours	Soy, rice, barley, corn, whole wheat, potato, green split pea, lentil.
	Storage Tips: Store in cool, dry pantry for up to one month. After that, refrigerate. Corn meal must be refrigerated right away.
Baking powder	Aluminum-free such as Royal, Rumford, Price, Schillings. Low-sodium cereal-free by Cellu and Featherweight.
Thickeners	Arrowroot (also known as kuzu), quick tapioca, instant mashed potatoes, oat bran (Barbara's). Arrowroot is suggested because it adds extra calcium to foods and is easily digested.
Beans	Fresh, frozen, or well-drained canned. Garbanzo (chick pea), navy, lima,

pinto, black, split pea, lentil, soy, adzuki, black-eyed pea.

Storage Tips:
Store in air-tight glass containers away from light and heat.

Soups Defatted chicken broth, lentil, split pea, minestrone, turkey rice (Health Valley, Walnut Acres).

Flavor extracts Pure almond, coconut, maple, anise, lemon, lime, orange, rum, vanilla (Bickford Flavors). Vanilla and almond together taste like butterscotch.

Herbs, spices and condiments Fresh or dried garlic, parsley, mustard, cayenne pepper, red pepper, black pepper, chili pepper, fennel, dill, horseradish, oregano, basil, sage, savory, rosemary, cumin, curry, ginger, tarragon, cinnamon, thyme, nutmeg, allspice, Chinese five-spice. Tabasco sauce, Worcestershire sauce, and Dijon mustard, Angostura bitters, capers.

Storage Tips:
Store dried herbs and spices in a cool place rather than above your stove where heat can affect them. The refrigerator or freezer tends to dry them out too much. A cool environment protects the volatile oils from warmth and moisture that change aromatic and pungent flavors.

Vinegars Rice, wine, champagne, apple cider, raspberry, Balsamic, herb blends.

Salt Sea salt or solar-evaporated salt (De Souza).

Sweeteners Raw, unheated honey, maple syrup, maple granules, date sugar; unsweetened fruit juices used sparingly for added flavors. Carob Dream (Choice Creations).

Avoid all artificial sweeteners, including aspartame.

Beverages
Herbal teas such as lemon grass, mint, pau d'areo, hibiscus, chamomile, rosehips, fennel, or taheebo (good for yeast problems); sparkling mineral waters.

Pure water is the best beverage of all. A good water filter that removes harmful bacteria and chemical pollutants is a necessity in this day and age. Seagull IV is the filter I personally use and suggest to my patients. University studies have shown this to be one of the best available on the market today.

Coffee substitutes
Dakopa (made from dahlia flower tubers), dandelion coffee, Pero, Postum, Pioneer, Bambu.

Alcohol
For cooking and moderate drinking, use sulfite-free wines (Domaine de la Bousquette and Frey), vermouth, sherry, and Pernod. Vodka and sake (rice wine) for allergic individuals. Fruit liqueurs such as amaretto (almond), Grand Marnier (orange and cognac), Cointreau (orange), creme de menthe (mint), kirsch (sherry), and creme de cassis (black currant) enhance special desserts.

Gelatin
Agar-agar, a seaweed gelatin, replaces animal gelatin. Agar-agar provides added fiber and lubrication in the intestinal tract by absorbing moisture (Westbrae).

Food Sources

- Spicer's International, P.O. Box 99, Oglesby, IL 61348. (1-800-824-3196)

Water Filter Source

- General Ecology Inc., 151 Sheree Bl., Lionville, PA 19353

- de Buren's Optimum I Hypoallergenic Vitamin Mineral Supplement, 35 Via Los Altos, Tiburon, CA 94920 (415-383-1405)

Special note: For low-sodium dieters, the Diamond Crystal Salt Company has introduced a line of specialty foods for modified diets. They feature single-serving, heat-and-serve pouch entrees that require no freezing or refrigeration. "Back to Basics" entrees are gourmet-tasting without the fats, salt, and sugar so commonly associated with high-flavor convenience foods. Be aware, however, that wheat flour and milk are used in several of the protein entrees. Nonetheless, Back to Basics is a cut above the frozen entrees currently on the market. The various beef, chicken, shrimp, and chili dishes are satisfying and nutritious.

- Diamond Crystal, 10 Burlington Ave., Wilmington, MA 01887 (1-800-225-0592)

A Cleansing Formula

For the past ten years, I have personally used and recommended this formula for elimination of food sprays, bacteria, fungus, parasites, and heavy metals without any report of adverse reaction. Military families stationed in Turkey, China, and Southeast Asia have also used it through the suggestion of the U.S. State Department. However, it is just as valuable and just as necessary here in America, where so many pesticides and chemical wastes are entering our food supply. Clorox kills every known type of virus. If you're worried about the epidemic of salmonella in chickens, this treatment is the solution.

The following advantages have been reported over the years:

1. Allergic reaction is eliminated.
2. Fruits and vegetables taste "farm fresh" and keep twice as long.
3. Leafy greens retain their color and crispness.
4. Meats are tenderized with flavors enhanced.

The Formula

1. Use ½ teaspoon Clorox to 1 gallon of water, obtained from the usual source. Only the Clorox brand will work, so do not substitute any other product.
2. Place the foods to be treated into the bath according to the chart below. Make a separate bath for each group.
3. Remove foods from the Clorox bath and place in clear water for ten minutes. Dry all foods thoroughly, and store.

Food Group	Treatment Time
Vegetables	
Leafy vegetables	15 minutes
Root vegetables, thick-skinned or fibrous vegetables	30 minutes
Fruits	
Thin-skinned berries, peaches, apricots, plums	15 minutes
Thick-skinned fruits such as apples, citrus, and bananas	30 minutes
Chicken, fish, meats, eggs	20 minutes

Note: Meats can be thawed in a Clorox bath. The timing is about 20 minutes for a weight of 2 to 5 pounds. Frozen turkey or chicken should remain in the Clorox bath until thawed. Ground meats, of course, cannot be Cloroxed.

Mail Order Suppliers of Organic Food

The following growers and distributors can ship their products directly, usually via UPS, and do not require a minimum order unless otherwise noted.

To minimize shipping costs, it pays to order from a farm close to home and in large quantities. If any of these growers are in your area, you may want to visit their farms. You can also call to find out which retail stores in your area carry their products.

Please note that when the products are "certified organic" they are done so by an independent agency. The "self certified" farms or distributors are self-regulated and growers are often required to substantiate that the farming practices are organic.

Arizona

Arjoy Acres
HCR Box 1410
Payson, AZ 85541
(602-474-1224)

Garlic, elephant garlic, shallots. *Not* certified.

Pine Ridge Farms
P.O. Box 98
Subiaco, AR 72865
(501-934-4565)

Chicken, turkey, and beef (beef is not given drugs, but feed is not organic). Certified organic.

Arkansas

Mountain Ark Trading
  Company
120 South East Ave.
Fayetteville, AR 72701
(800-643-8909)

Macrobiotic foods, vegetables, miso, seasonings, rice, pasta, fruit, spreads, oils, beans, soup. Self-certified.

California

Lee Anderson's
  Covaldo Date Co.
P.O. Box 908
Coachella, CA 92236
(619-398-3441)
Mon–Fri 9–12; 1–4:30

Dates, pecans, citrus, figs, raisins. Self-certified.

Living Tree Centre
P.O. Box 797
Bolinas, CA 94924
(415-868-2224)

Almonds, almond butter, silverskin garlic, red Jerusalem artichokes, various vegetable seed. Artichokes and seeds are certified organic by the California Certified Organic Farmers.

Timber Crest Farms
4791 Dry Creek Road
Healdsburg, CA 95448
(707-433-8251)

A wide variety of dried fruits. *Not* certified.

Joe Soghomonian
8624 S. Chestnut
Fresno, CA 93725
(209-834-2772)

Grapes and walnuts in season only, raisins year-round. Certified organic by California Certified Organic Farmers.

West Valley Produce
  Co.
726 South Mateo St.
Los Angeles, CA 90021
(213-627-4131 or
  629-1656)

A variety of fruits and vegetables. Most products are certified organic by California Certified Organic Farmers.

Be Wise Ranch
Bill Brammar
9018 Artesian Road
San Diego, CA 92127
(619-756-4851)

Limes, lemons, avocados, oranges. Certified organic by California Certified Organic Farmers. A minimum order of 40 pounds of citrus and 25 pounds of avocados is required.

Sun Mountain
  Research Center
35751 Oak Springs Drive
Tollhouse, CA 93667
(209-855-3710)

Herbs, herb seeds. Certified organic by California Certified Organic Farmers.

G & J Farms
Gregory F. Gaffney
4218 W. Muscat
Fresno, CA 93706
(209-268-2835)

Apricots, peaches, assorted vegetables. Certified organic by California Certified Organic Farmers.

Ecology Sound Farms
42126 Road 168
Orosi, CA 93647
(209-528-3816)

Kiwi, persimmons, Asian pears, plums, oranges, garlic, dried fruit. Certified organic.

Giusto's Specialty
  Foods, Inc.
241 East Harris Ave., S
San Francisco, CA 94080
(415-873-6566)

Breads, cakes, grains, spices, cereals, flours, oils, seeds, cookies, yeast. *Not* certified.

Jaffe Brothers
P.O. Box 636
Valley Center,
  CA 92082-0636
(619-749-1133)

Dried fruits, nuts, brown rice, pasta, oils, grains and cereals. Requires growers to fill out farming practice surveys. Self-certified.

Canada

Oak Manor Farms
Tavistock, Ontario
Canada N0B 2R0
(519-662-2385)

Flours, grains, beans, seeds, cereals, coffee. Certified organic.

Connecticut

Butterbrooke Farm
78 Barry Road
Oxford, CT 06483
(203-888-2000)

Seventy-five varieties of chemically untreated, open-pollinated, short-maturity seeds. *Not* certified.

Idaho

Brown Company
P.O. Box 69
Tetonia, ID 83452
(208-456-2500 or
   456-2629)

Idaho potatoes, seed potatoes. *Not* certified.

Iowa

Frontier Cooperative
   Herbs
P.O. Box 299
Norway, IO 52318
(319-227-7991)

Herbs and spices. Certified organic.

Maryland

Smile Herb Shop
4908 Berwyn Road
College Park, MD 20740
(301-474-4288 or
   474-8495)

A variety of fruits and vegetables. Most products are certified organic by the Organic Crop Improvement Association.

Tuscarora Valley Beef
   Farm
P.O. Box 15839
Chevy Chase, MD 20815
(301-588-5220)

Lamb, veal, beef, nitrite-free bacon, and lower-fat chicken sausages. *Not* certified.

Michigan

Eugene and Joan Saintz
2225 63rd St.
Fennville, MI 49408
(616-561-2761)

A variety of in-season fruits and vegetables. Certified organic by the Organic Growers of Michigan.

American Spoon Foods
411 E. Lake St.
Petoskey, MI 49770
(616-347-9030)

Pancake and waffle mix made with organically grown Indian blue corn, wild rice, wild berry preserves, wild pecans. *Not* certified.

Country Life Natural Foods
109 Avenue
Pullman, MI 49450
(616-236-5011)

Beans, grains, seeds, nuts, raisins. Certain products are certified.

Minnesota

Diamond K Enterprises
R.R. 1, Box 30
St. Charles, MN 55972
(507-932-4308)

Grains, flour, cereal, pancake mixes, nuts, dried fruits, alfalfa seeds. Self-certified.

Living Farms
Box 50
Tracey, MN 56175
(800-622-5235—MN)
(800-533-5320—out-of-state)

Grains, beans, rice, wheat, sunflowers, sprouting alfalfa, clover, and radishes. Self-certified.

Midheaven Farms Beef
Rt. 1, Box 404
Park Rapids, MN 56470
(218-732-4866)

Beef. Certified organic by the Minnesota Organic Growers Association. Will ship directly to consumers in the Minnesota area and can refer consumers to retailers of certified organic beef in the Twin Cities, Wisconsin, South Dakota, North Dakota, and parts of Montana.

New York

Chesnok Farm
R.D. #1, Marshland Road
Apalachin, NY 13732
(607-748-3495)

Shallots, garlic. *Not* certified.

Four Chimneys Farm Winery
R.D. #1, Hall Road
Himrod, NY 14842
(607-243-7502)

Wine, grape juice, wine vinegar, champagne. Certified organic by Natural Food Associates of NY. Alcohol can be shipped only within New York State.

Deer Valley Farm
R.D. 1
Guilford, NY 13780
(607-764-8556)

Beef, chicken, turkey, pork, eggs, cheeses (nonorganic), fruit, flowers, grains, herbs, juices, pasta, oils, soups, soap, spreads, spaghetti, vitamins, sugar, seasonings, baked goods, confections, nuts. Certified organic.

Ohio

Millstream Marketing
1310A East Tallmadge
   Ave.
Cuyahoga Falls, OH
(216-630-2700)

A variety of fruits and vegetables shipped within a 150-mile radius of Akron. Some products are certified.

Pennsylvania

Garden Spot
   Distributors
Rt. 1, Box 729A
New Holland, PA 17557
(800-292-9631—PA)
(800-445-5100—
   northeastern U.S.)
(717-354-4936—local)

Baked goods, cereals, dried fruits, nuts, seeds, grains, flours, beans, granola, teas, herbs, pet foods. Self-certified.

Neshaminy Valley
   Natural Foods
421 Pike Road
Huntingdon Valley, PA
   19006
(215-364-8440)

Popcorn, grains, beans, dried fruit, pasta, flours, cereals, seeds, unsprayed nuts, miso, candies, teas, pickles, and some macrobiotic products. Only a buying club of six households or more can order products. Self-certified.

Rising Sun Distributors
P.O. Box 627
Milesburg, PA 16853
(814-355-9850)

Beef, poultry, lamb, pork, fruits, vegetables, beans, seeds, and grains. Certified organic.

Walnut Acres
Penns Creek, PA 17862
(717-837-0601)

Meat, fish, poultry, canned vegetables, cheeses, grains, seeds, flours, nuts, pasta, seasonings, dried fruit, juices, salad dressings, granola, and peanut butter. Self-certified.

Vermont

Hill and Dale Farms
West Hill–Daniel Davis
   Road
Putney, VT 05346
(802-387-5817)

Apples and vinegar. (Company expects to be certified organic by winter of 1987.)

Virginia

Golden Acres Orchard
A.P. Thomson
Rt. 2, Box 2450
Front Royal, VA 22630
(703-636-9611)

Apples in season, apple cider vinegar, apple juice. Self-certified.

Jordan River Farm
Huntly, VA 22640
(703-636-9388)

Grass-fed beef, free-range eggs from healthier chickens raised on an open range instead of in small enclosed coops, and, occasionally, organic veal. Self-certified.

Washington

Homestead Organic
   Produce
Bill Weiss
Rt. 1, 2002 Road 7, N.W.
Quincy, WA 98848
(509-787-2248)

Gourmet sweet onions. Certified organic by Washington State Tilth Producer's Cooperative. A 10-pound minimum order is required.

Cascadian Farm
Star Route
Rockport, WA 98283
(206-853-8175)

Fruit conserves and dill pickles. Certified organic.

The Meat Shop, Inc.
6522 Freemon Ave.
  North
Seattle, WA 98103
(206-789-5834)

Meat. Producers must sign an affidavit certifying that they use no antibiotics and animals are not given drugs, but feed is not organic. *Not* certified.

West Virginia

Hardscrabble
  Enterprises, Inc.
Paul and Nan Goland
Route 6, Box 42
Cherry Grove, WV 26804
(304-567-2727)

Oak (Shiitake) mushrooms. *Not* certified.

Brier Run Farm
Rt. 1, Box 73
Birch River, WV 26610
(304-649-2975)

Soft goat's cheese. No animal drugs used, but feed is not organic. *Not* certified.

Special Salad Dressings

There are now special salad dressings on the market which are quite similar to the recipes used in this book. These dressings can be obtained from:

Life Design Products
P.O. Box 3749
Batesville, AR 72503
(800-348-6060 x325)

A Note About Irradiated Food

There is a controversy about the safety of eating irradiated food, a process that extends shelf life by using ionizing radiation. Aside from the questionable safety factor, I personally feel that since there are so many conditions in our society today that devitalize and contaminate food, I am not in favor of adding another one. If you want further information on this topic contact: The Health and Energy Institute, 236 Massachusetts Ave. N.E., Washington, D.C. 20002, (202-543-1070).

14

ABOUT THE DIET: QUESTIONS AND ANSWERS

The food you eat today, walks around tomorrow.
—Dr. Hazel Parcells

Q. Is fruit a major part of the food plan as it is in recent popular diets?

A. No.

A *maximum* of three fruit portions per day is the most you should consume. A portion equals one-half grapefruit, for example, or ten cherries, one medium peach, one small orange, two medium prunes, or twelve grapes. (See Food Equivalents on p. 202 for a complete list.)

I have reviewed too many diet histories and coordinating blood values not to notice that people who eat large amounts of fruit have high triglyceride values and a disturbed calcium balance. With more medical attention focused on preventing osteoporosis, a degenerative bone disease that affects 15 to 20 million postmenopausal American women, it makes good nutritional sense to cut out calcium-lowering sugar and limit even natural sugar sources from excess fruit, for example, and even fruit juice.

In addition to unbalancing mineral ratios in the body, excessive sugar can also block essential fat conversion into prostaglandins. Essential fat itself helps to maintain calcium levels in the blood by delivering it to the soft tissues.

Vegetarians, I have often observed, will eat an entire meal of only fruit. They should concentrate instead on more protein-rich beans and whole grains for balanced nourishment.

The body does not differentiate between the sources of sugar. Too much of a sweet thing—whether refined or natural—can result in problems, so all sweets, *including fruit*, should be monitored. Excessive sugar consumption is often connected with dental cavities, diabetes, depression, hypoglycemia, and hyperactivity. It may also lower resistance to viruses and colds, or depress immune system response.

Q. I am on a low-salt diet. Is the New Nutrition Diet sodium-restricted?

A. Yes.

The New Nutrition Master Plan is also a controlled sodium diet containing less than 1500 mg. of sodium per day. The use of added salt is optional in all of the recipes; however, even with the added salt, the total daily amount does not exceed 1500 mg. If you do choose to omit the salt, use a suitable salt substitute to preserve flavor. Excessive sodium consumption may contribute to high blood pressure and water retention. Both the preferred salt and sweetening choices have been listed under "Stocking and Storing the Staples" (p. 120).

Q. Are dairy products recommended?

A. Dairy products are permitted, but not recommended.

Homogenized whole or low-fat milk products are not allowed because of the presence of the destructive enzyme xanthine oxidase (XO). XO has been associated with artery damage, and is easily absorbed by the body in the dispersed milkfat. Low-fat milk (2 percent) is not allowed either, because it derives over 30 percent of its calories from homogenized milkfat. Nonfat milk, cheese, and yogurt are permitted because technically they contain no fat. If you suspect a sensitivity to dairy products or experience sinus problems, I suggest you eliminate all dairy items from the diet. One of the insidious effects of food sensitivity is weight gain due to retention of fluid (edema) because of an inflammatory reaction in the tissues.

Goat milk, cheese, and yogurt are recommended as the ideal dairy sources because they are not homogenized. They are also better tolerated by many individuals, hence less allergenic, than milk products from cows. There are many first-rate goat cheeses now available, since goat cheese production in the United States has increased in the last few years.

Yogurt cheese is a deliciously simple snack. Nutmeg, cinnamon, cardamom, or vanilla extract can add an extra dash of flavor. You will need to make the yogurt cheese one day ahead. The recipe calls for just 1 cup (one 8-ounce container) of nonfat yogurt. Pour the yogurt into a cheesecloth-lined colander that is set over a bowl. Cover and refrigerate for 24 hours. You will have ½ cup of yogurt cheese in a day.

Q. What about coffee?
A. No.

Coffee is not recommended because it contains caffeine, a detrimental nerve stimulant, and irritating volatile oils. Caffeine stimulates the adrenal glands, causing adrenalin to be released into the bloodstream. Adrenalin activates our fight-or-flight response, increasing our heart rate, blood pressure, and blood sugar. When this initial rush wears off, blood sugar drops to lower levels than before the coffee and leaves the adrenal glands in a depleted state. And then it's time for another cup of coffee.

When sugar is added, the problem is intensified because refined sugars have the same stressful effect on the adrenal glands. Frequent use of coffee exhausts the adrenal glands and probably is the most central factor in low blood sugar in coffee drinkers. This also applies to chocolate, which contains caffeine and a related substance, theobromine.

Coffee may also irritate sensitive intestinal membranes.

It interferes with the absorption of minerals, especially magnesium and iron. It depletes vitamins B and C, and alters the balance of neurotransmitters in the brain. University studies have shown that drinking more than two cups of coffee per day also elevates cholesterol levels.

Decaffeinated coffee also has detrimental effects on the body. Some decaffeination processes leave chemical residues such as methylene chloride, which is toxic to the liver and causes cancer in laboratory animals. Water extraction or Swiss process decaffeination is safer; however, most of the negative effects of coffee remain. Whether decaffeinated or not, imported coffees contain insecticide residues that are prohibited in this country.

Q. What about alcohol?
A. Yes.
Alcohol can be used in cooking but not consumed as a beverage. Moderate to heavy alcohol consumption blocks prostaglandin production. Wine and sherry are used in the recipes because, when used for cooking, most of the alcohol is burned off while the flavor remains. Alcohol burn-off takes about half an hour when food is simmering in soups and stews. It burns off in three minutes when used to sauté.

While there is evidence that it may raise beneficial HDL cholesterol levels, taken straight and in excessive amounts (more than a couple of beers, two small glasses of wine, or two mixed drinks), alcohol can have detrimental effects on the body. It interferes with the utilization of the essential fatty acids; it can prematurely age the skin, causing drying, wrinkling, and loss of elasticity. Other medical problems of excessive alcohol use include cirrhosis of the liver (fatty liver), malnutrition (empty calories, reduced stomach-acid secretion, altered digestive system), depression, and blood sugar instability.

Grain-sensitive individuals may react badly to alcoholic beverages derived from grains such as wheat, rye, corn, barley, and hops. If you suspect that you are one of these individuals, use vodka (from potatoes) or sake (rice wine). The sulfite preservative used in most wines can also have ill effects on asthmatic, allergic, and sensitive individuals.

Some alcoholism is genetically based. Certain races (such as the American Indians) or families with a history of alcoholism have a defective liver enzyme that metabolizes alcohol. Such people experience irritation of the nervous system and intense cravings for more alcohol. These individuals should completely avoid all alcohol.

Q. Are soft drinks allowed?
A. No.
Soft drinks are not recommended because they contain refined sugar or sugar substitutes such as aspartame (NutraSweet) or saccharine. Refined sugar depletes the body of B vitamins and unbalances calcium/phosphorus ratios.

Sugar substitutes such as saccharine have been known to cause liver damage to test animals at high doses. Aspartame, the most recently developed sugar substitute, is composed of the two amino acids phenylalanine and aspartic acid, and wood alcohol (methanol). It has been implicated in a wide range of complaints, including seizures, high blood pressure, and visual impairment.

Q. Do you suggest extra vitamins and minerals?
A. Yes.
The inclusion of a multivitamin and mineral supplement that contains the necessary co-factors for essential fat conversion is a dietary necessity for several reasons:

1. It is included because without the necessary vitamins— such as niacin, B-6, C, zinc, and magnesium— GLA and EPA cannot convert into the protective prostaglandins. Weight loss also may be inhibited. I suggest using a supplement to assure the inclusion of the essential vitamins and minerals because food sources for these nutrients may be unreliable due to topsoil depletion (zinc), food processing (depletes B-6 and magne-

sium), and storage time (vitamin C) before the food gets to your table.

2. The nutrient tables from agricultural handbooks, or such an esteemed nutritional reference as Bowes and Church's *Food Values of Portions Commonly Used*, are not accurate reflections of how much nutrition is in our foods when we eat them. The vitamin and mineral levels are determined right after food has been harvested. These levels do not reflect the decrease in value by the canning process, in which up to 80 percent of vitamins are lost, or by freezing, in which up to 45 percent of vitamins are lost.

3. Then there is environmental pollution that creates a vitamin and mineral deficit. Each year we are exposed to 200,000 tons of air pollutants per person, and ingest 5 pounds of food additives and 120 pounds of sugar. In addition, there is the massive variety of pesticides and industrial wastes in both water and food. These substances deplete nutrients from our bodies in the process of detoxifying and eliminating them. Pollution necessitates more vitamins A, C, and E. Smoking destroys 25 mg. of vitamin C *per cigarette*. Chlorinated drinking water eats up more vitamin E, and glaring fluorescent office lights strain the body's supply of vitamin A.

4. Medications such as aspirin, cold remedies, and tranquilizers cancel out nutrients. Birth control pills create a need for additional B-6 and B-12, as well as folic acid. Alcohol eliminates the B vitamins, and a lack of thiamin (vitamin B-1) is linked to marginal malnutrition similar to beriberi among today's adolescents, who eat excessive amounts of junk food.

5. Psychological stress can require increased supplementation of one or more nutrients. The *American Physician Family Journal* advises that "all recent surveys indicate that Americans lack calcium, iron, magnesium, B-6, and zinc" —three of the five necessities for good-fat utilization.

Consult your nutritionally oriented doctor for more

specific guidance beyond the multiple vitamin/mineral supplement suggested here. (I recommend de Buren's Optimum I Supplement—see page 128.) Remember that vitamins in mega amounts act like drugs on the body. The same pharmacological effects can be experienced with herbs, because herbs are the original "medicants" from which modernday drugs are derived. Digitalis comes from foxglove, and belladonna from the herb by the same name. Valium is a derivative of the valerian root, and aspirin has its roots in willow bark. So be careful when using any of these without professional guidance.

Q. Why are portions given for fruit and protein if weight loss is not the concern?

A. In order to get the most out of the New Nutrition Diet, you need to understand the chemistry behind it. The specific amounts (i.e., 4 ounces or ½ cup) of fruit and protein must be followed exactly as shown because of their connection with mineral balance that affects the prostaglandins. Too much fruit can create mineral loss by upsetting the calcium/phosphorus ratio, which in turn depletes other available minerals that are needed as co-factors in prostaglandin metabolism. Similarly, excess protein can drain the body's mineral reserves, depleting the available minerals used for prostaglandins.

Q. What should be limited for weight loss?

A. If you are overweight or inactive, and have not been using unrefined oils or supplementing with GLA directly, you are not adequately metabolizing high-calorie foods. This is why daily amounts of cereals, breads, starchy vegetables, and beans are also given—but in parentheses, because not everybody needs to lose weight. After the initial three-week phase, portions given in the parentheses can be increased in ½ cup increments until you can eat all you want without gaining weight.

Remember that when your fat burner is normalized and nutritionally sustained with the unrefined vegetable oils and/or preformed GLA supplements, appetite will naturally decrease and you will be satisfied with smaller portions. You will not have to resort to will-power or tedious calorie counting to prevent overeating.

Balanced metabolism is the goal. The elimination of sugar, trans fats, and alcohol will not only allow the oils to help you metabolize greater calories, it will prevent dips in blood sugar levels that cause you to overeat.

Q. How does butter figure into the diet?
A. The use of additional butter to the diet, other than the trace amounts contained in certain recipes in the menu, is not recommended until weight loss has been stabilized. Although butter can theoretically be desig-nated a healthy fat when eaten in moderation, it does not contain enough of the cis-linoleic fatty acid to con-vert to fat-burning GLA and therefore cannot assist in initial weight loss. Once weight loss is maintained, but-ter can be added in the amounts of 1 to 2 teaspoons per meal as long as the unrefined oils are still included in equal amounts.

The New Nutrition Diet Master Menu Plan is de-signed to be safe for everybody in every respect. Variety is a key feature of the plan, so you will note that the same foods are not repeated every day. Variety eating thereby ensures the consumption of a wide range of vegetables, fruits, protein, and complex carbohydrates. This gives the body maximum exposure to all fifty nutri-ents from food sources. Mother Nature has blessed us with more than sixty varieties of vegetables and more than twenty kinds of fruits and beans. When meals are planned according to nutritional value and appeal, color inevitably comes into play. Colorful meals provide par-ticular nutritional assistance. In foods colored orange and yellow, vitamin A is highlighted; red and blue foods provide iron-rich nutrition, while green foods give us magnesium.

From the overweight to the allergic to the high-risk cardiovascular patient to the individual wanting to improve his or her immune system—everyone can enjoy the fruits of the New Nutrition system.

The Ten-Point Prescription

The Ten-Point Prescription is a summary of the New Nutritional approach. These ten practical guidelines are designed for sustained weight loss and long-term health.

1. Eliminate all sources of damaged fats, such as commercial vegetable oils, hydrogenated oil products (margarine and vegetable shortening), and all products containing them (read the labels). Use only purified, unrefined, expeller-pressed, raw or virgin oils.

2. Avoid dried, cured, and aged animal foods (powdered milk, dried eggs, and aged cheese such as Parmesan).

3. Eliminate whole or low-fat homogenized cow's milk, yogurt, and cheese. Nonfat dairy products, in which there is no fat content, are permitted. Goat's milk, yogurt, and cheese are acceptable.

4. At fast food restaurants, avoid hot dogs, hamburgers, bacon, chicken, french fries and onion rings, fish, mayonnaise, salad dressings, sauces, and sodas. It's okay to have a salad if you bring your own essential-fat dressing.

5. Consume at least three fish meals per week (favor salmon, mackerel, sardines, tuna, trout, cod, crab, and shrimp).

6. Include two tablespoons of essential fat every day in salad dressings and cooking. (Use only olive, canola, or peanut oil when cooking.)

7. Include up to but not more than three whole, portion-controlled fruits per day.

8. Eat high-fiber oats, beans, vegetables, and fruits.

9. Use onion, garlic, lemon, herbs, flavor extracts, and alcohol in cooking to season food. To prevent yeast problems, limit mustards, vinegars, tomato sauces, and soy sauce.

10. Drink at least eight glasses of water per day from sources such as spring, mineral, or filtered. Herbal tea or coffee substitutes should be made from these waters.

15

THE TWO-WEEK
FAT FLUSH

*The human body has one ability not
possessed by any machine—
the ability to repair itself.*
—GEORGE E. KRILEY, JR., M.D.

The Two-Week Fat Flush is a quick way to cleanse the
accumulated bad fats in the tissues and liver. It also
prevents new fats, in the form of triglycerides, from
forming and reestablishes a beneficial fat ratio in the
brown fat tissues for continued weight stabilization,
fat-burning stimulation, and appetite control.

Some people lose up to 10 inches at the waist, buttocks, and thighs, whereas they may lose only 5 pounds
on the scale. This two-week plan flushes out fat that
normal diets don't. On this companion program to the
New Nutrition Diet Master Strategy, you will lose weight
and begin to metabolize the toxic water and fat accu-
mulation in your body.

If you are doing the program mainly for weight loss,
weigh yourself only once a week. People do not lose
weight at the same rate and you can get discouraged if
you hit a plateau. You can completely redistribute your
weight on this program without a dramatic loss on the
scale.

Give Your Liver a Vacation

The *fat flush* gives the liver a well-deserved vacation from its many functions. The liver synthesizes and normalizes blood protein, stores glycogen, normalizes blood fats, and manufactures bile to digest dietary fats and oils. It detoxifies the blood from chemicals, drugs, and bacteria of all types. A liver clogged with poisons or excess fats cannot perform its essential duties.

The Fat Flush Program

The foods to be consumed for breakfast, lunch, and dinner are from the following food groups only. The list is restricted to whole natural foods without salt, spices, vinegar, mustards, or herbs. These seasonings can create water retention and yeast infections. The Two-Week Fat Flush can help diminish these problems as well, so you will find the food choices pure and simple:

Oil	*1 tablespoon twice daily.* Select unrefined or expeller-pressed safflower oil, which has the highest fat-burning potential.
Lean protein	(up to 8 ounces per day) All varieties of fish, lean beef, veal, lamb, skinless chicken, and turkey.
Vegetables	Unlimited raw or steamed. Choose from high-fiber selections: asparagus, green beans, broccoli, brussels sprouts, cabbage, cauliflower, Chinese cabbage, cucumbers, eggplant, escarole, lettuce, okra, onions, parsley, green and red bell peppers, radishes, mung bean sprouts, tomatoes, watercress, zucchini, yellow squash, water chestnuts, bamboo shoots, garlic.

Fruits	*2 whole portions daily.* Choose from: 1 small apple, ½ banana, ½ grapefruit, 1 small orange, 2 medium plums, 6 large strawberries, 1 slice fresh pineapple, 10 large cherries, 1 nectarine.

While there are many other fruits available, these choices produce the best results because they are not as concentrated in fruit sugar as other varieties and so do not promote overconsumption.

Long Life Cocktail	(to increase elimination) 1 teaspoon of powdered psyllium husks in 8 ounces unsweetened cranberry juice or cranberry juice sweetened with grape concentrate (available in health food stores), taken when you wake up and before bedtime. (Metamucil is a popular brand available in most pharmacies.)

Besides the Daily Diet

- **With or between meals**

  Drink an 8-ounce cup of hot water with juice of ½ lemon twice a day to assist kidney and liver elimination.

- **Breakfast and dinner**

  Take supplements rich in fat-burning GLA. Choose from plain GLA supplement (90 mg.) and take 2 capsules twice daily, or choose evening primrose oil (500 mg.) and take 4 capsules twice daily.

- Take a balanced multivitamin/mineral supplement.

- Drink an additional 6 glasses of pure room-temperature water per day. Room temperature is best for digestion because extremely hot or extra cold or iced drinks depress gastric juices.

- Cranberry juice contains several digestive enzymes not found in other foods. To make cranberry juice yourself, here's a simple recipe: Put 1 pound of fresh cranberries into a large saucepan. Add 5 cups of water. Boil until all berries pop. Strain juice and add a touch of grape concentrate to take the edge off the tartness. Brave souls can take it straight.

- Additional water will assist in diluting the increased body wastes from the detoxification process. Spring water or filtered water is the preferred source. Distilled water is *not* recommended because it can leach minerals from the body, notably calcium, and can result in a weakened heart muscle. The water should be taken consistently throughout the day, but avoid drinking during meals so that digestive juices are not diluted. Remember that drinking adequate amounts of water is essential to weight loss.

Metabolizing stored fat into energy for the body is the liver's most important function. This water flush will allow the liver to operate at optimum potential and speed up its metabolic removal of stored fats, resulting in healthy weight loss.

Detox While Dieting

Weight loss must always accompany a detoxification program. Body fat stores environmental toxins from chemicals and pesticides in food, air, and water as well as PCB's and auto exhaust. Fat can be burned off by eating the proper foods and exercising, but the toxins are generally not burned in the usual weight-loss regimen. Unburned poisons often relocate from the shrinking fat reserves to the bloodstream, organs, and tissues, causing discomfort such as headaches and nausea. Therefore, it is imperative to deal with these toxins while dieting. My Two Week Fat Flush program does this very effectively by increasing oil, water, and exercise.

There is a twofold reason for following the daily tablespoon oil requirement:

1. Oil has GLA fat burning potential, and
2. Oil attracts the oil soluble poisons which have been lodged in the fatty tissues of the body and carries them out of the system for elimination.

Daily Exercise

Especially important at this time is daily moderate aerobic exercise for at least 20 to 30 minutes to keep the released toxins moving.

The Water Connection

Since water is the most natural and effective diluting agent, it is important that it be used therapeutically for cleansing. Drinking any other liquids, such as coffee, tea (even herbal teas), soft drinks, diet drinks, carbonated water, mineral water, or unsweetened fruit juices, is not recommended at this time. All of these beverages contain some type of substance that must go through a digestive process. This is exactly what you don't want.

- Drinking water before a meal takes the edge off the appetite.

- Water ensures normal bowel and kidney function to rid the body of wastes as well as stored fat.

- Drinking water alleviates fluid retention, since only when the body gets plenty of water will it release the stored water.

- Water gets rid of excess salt.

- Water helps plump the skin and prevents dehydration.

- Water helps to prevent the sagging skin conditions that often follow weight loss.

Adequate amounts of water will assist the kidneys to filter their own waste products so the liver can begin to metabolize its own waste products without having to do the kidneys' work.

Putting It All Together

A sample day from a client's diet diary on the Fat Flush Program looks like this:

Upon arising	Long Life Cocktail
	30 minute brisk walk
Before Breakfast	8 ounces hot water with lemon juice
Breakfast	8 ounces steamed broccoli with red peppers
	2 90 mg. GLA capsules
	1 multivitamin/mineral tablet
	8 ounces water
Mid-morning	1 small orange
20 minutes before lunch	1 8-ounce glass water
Lunch	4 ounces broiled swordfish with parsley and garlic
	Large green leafy salad with chives, sprouts, shredded cabbage, and water chestnuts
	1 tablespoon safflower oil
	1 8-ounce glass water
Mid-afternoon	2 8-ounce glasses water
4:00 P.M.	½ banana
20 minutes before dinner	1 8-ounce glass water
Dinner	4 ounces baked chicken with tomatoes and onions
	4 ounces steamed asparagus
	Raw cucumber and radish-slice salad
	1 tablespoon safflower oil

2 90 mg. GLA capsules
8 ounces hot water with lemon
juice

Mid-evening   Long Life Cocktail

What It Means for You

You can use this example as a basic menu guide. Just substitute foods from the same food groups for daily variety. The time frame for the Long Life Cocktail, hot water with lemon, and GLA and multivitamin/mineral supplementation can remain the same as provided in the sample guide. You can change the fluid intake to suit your schedule if that is more convenient, of course.

A Gentle Reminder: Especially for This Two-Week Period

No herbs, spices, vinegar, mustard, or soy sauce.

No trans fat.

No alcohol.

No sugar.

No oils or fats of any kind other than the daily salad oil and the good-fat supplements.

No grains, bread, cereal, or starchy vegetables such as beans, potatoes, corn, parsnips, carrots, peas, pumpkin, or acorn or butternut squash.

No eggs or dairy products such as milk or cheese.

Seasonal Tune-up

This two-week cleansing diet is a marvelous body tune-up. You may want to consider doing this cleanse four times a year right before the seasons change. My patients usually will take the first two weeks of January, April, July, and October to get back on track and lose their fat.

Now you are ready for the next step.

16

THE NEW NUTRITION DIET PRESCRIPTION

Prepare simple meals, chew well, sup lightly.
—LEONARDO DA VINCI

Now you are ready to put all the dietary concepts of the New Nutrition together in an easy-to-follow daily plan. Here is the daily Master Formula that will ensure optimum nutrition.

The New Nutrition Diet Master Formula

1. 2 tablespoons essential-fat oil
2. 6 to 8 ounces protein
3. 4 or more vegetable servings
4. 1 to 3 fruit servings
5. 2 or more complex carbohydrate servings (starch)
6. 2 nonfat dairy servings (optional)
7. 2 90-mg. GLA supplements (4 90-mg. GLA for weight loss)
8. 3 280-mg. EPA supplements
9. Balanced multivitamin/mineral supplement

Do not eat   Trans fats (margarine, vegetable shortening, refined polyunsaturated oils)
              Refined carbohydrates (white flour, white sugar, cookies, candy, cake, soda)

Do not drink Alcohol

Do not compromise on trans fats, refined carbohydrates, or alcohol. These "foodless foods" can sabotage your health by blocking weight loss and prostaglandin production needed to regulate the cardiovascular, immune, and central nervous systems, as well as reproduction.

The Food Equivalents lists for essential and healthy fats, proteins, vegetables, fruits, complex carbohydrates, and dairy products (see pp. 202–208) will help you to choose the right portions for each serving of food, while reminding you of the great variety of foods available.

If you would like to follow a more specific plan, the 21-Day Master Menu is for you. The sample menus and recipes are based on the Master Formula. They are designed to omit dietary culprits such as damaged fats, excessively gluten-rich grains, fermented seasoning such as soy sauce, and the repetition of the same foods every day. By avoiding these dietary pitfalls, weight loss will be dramatic, digestion will improve, allergic edema will be eliminated, and the immune system will be strengthened.

If you are following the 21-Day Master Menu Plan, the Food Equivalents lists will also help you. You can switch any fruit or vegetable on the plan for another, provided you follow the recommended portion amounts for the substituted fruit or vegetable. For example, let's say that it is January and corn is on the menu. If you don't like frozen corn (frozen foods are allowed) but want a fresh seasonal vegetable instead, then look under the complex-carbohydrate list and find a vegetable that is in season— winter squash, for example. You can easily substitute ½ cup winter squash for the small ear of corn on the menu.

Whichever strategy you follow (the Master Formula to create your own food plan or the suggested menus) you can achieve excellent results. You might also decide simply to use some of the recipes in your own menu plan. That's fine, too.

21-Day Master Menu Plan

Following is a 21-day menu program to get you started eating the New Nutrition Diet way. Each menu incorporates the nutritional information outlined in the preceding chapters. Below are just a few guidelines to be followed daily:

- Recipes noted with an asterisk (*) appear in recipe section.

- For weight loss, follow amounts given in parentheses. Others may eat as much as they want.

- Beverages with meals include 1 cup herbal tea, mineral water, or coffee substitute.

- During this three week period snacks should be chosen from the 1 to 3 fruit servings (see p. 204). After this time you can substitute 1 Sweet Delight serving (pp. 194–201) for one of the fruit portions.

- When the fresh fruits and vegetables mentioned are not available, frozen vegetables and fruits, or fruits canned in their own juices, are suitable substitutes.

- For those wishing to avoid milk, see p. 208 for milk substitutes.

Week One—Monday

Breakfast	2 tablespoons apple butter in (½ cup) oatmeal ½ cup nonfat milk
Lunch	3 ounces canned or poached salmon with dill Warm asparagus Mixed green salad with *1 tablespoon Hazelnut Dressing (p. 169)

Dinner   4 ounces skinned roast turkey (white meat
          only)
          Baked cauliflower topped with
          *1 tablespoon Sesame Lemon Dressing
          (p. 171)
          (½ cup) baked winter squash with
          ¼ teaspoon vanilla extract and ⅛ teaspoon
          cinnamon

Week One—Tuesday

Breakfast   4 halves dried apricots chopped into
            (½ cup) cream of rye and
            4 ounces nonfat milk

Lunch   4 ounces lean broiled burger with sliced
            onions and parsley
            Green beans
            Sliced tomatoes with
            *1 tablespoon Walnut Raspberry Vinaigrette
            (p. 170)

Dinner   4 ounces shrimp with water chestnuts, car-
            rots, bok choy, and bean sprouts stir-
            sautéed in
            *1 tablespoon Peanut Dressing with Ginger
            and Garlic (p. 170)
            (½ cup) Chinese rice noodles

Week One—Wednesday

Breakfast   ½ banana sliced on
            (½ cup) cooked or (1 cup) puffed millet and
            4 ounces nonfat milk

Lunch   4 ounces curried tuna on sliced green pep-
            pers, radishes, and celery with
            *1 tablespoon French Olive Oil Dressing
            (p. 170)
            (½ cup) beets steamed with 2 small cinna-
            mon sticks

Dinner   *4 ounces Chicken with Sherry Dijon
          (p. 180)
         Baked chayote squash or zucchini topped
          with
         *1 tablespoon Sesame Lemon Dressing
          (p. 171)
         *Minted Carrots and Snow Peas (p. 193)

Week One—Thursday

Breakfast 1 small nectarine or peach
           2 soft- or hard-cooked eggs
           4 ounces nonfat milk

Lunch   *(1 cup) Sherried Black Bean Soup (p. 176)
           Steamed broccoli
           Radish and cucumber salad with
           *1 tablespoon Hazelnut Dressing (p. 169)

Dinner   *4 ounces Spiced Salmon Loaf (p. 186)
           *Bombay Curry Sauce (p. 171)
           Braised carrots and cabbage with
           ¼ teaspoon caraway seeds topped with
           *1 tablespoon Safflower Dressing with Pa-
            paya and Tarragon (p. 169)
           (½ cup) brown rice

Week One—Friday

Breakfast *1 Baked Apple with Raisins, Cinnamon, and
            Nutmeg (p. 195)
           (1 slice) rye toast with
           1 ounce tofu
           4 ounces nonfat milk

Lunch   3 ounces canned or broiled fresh mackerel
            fillets with salsa
           Sautéed red peppers and onions in white
            wine
           Green leafy salad with
           *1 tablespoon Sesame Lemon Dressing
            (p. 171)

Dinner 4 ounces broiled lamb chop with rosemary
Grilled eggplant and tomato garnish topped
with
*1 tablespoon French Olive Oil Dressing
(p. 170)
(¾ cup) steamed green peas

Week One—Saturday

Breakfast ½ cup blueberries
(½ cup) buckwheat groats (kasha) and
4 ounces nonfat milk

Lunch *6 tablespoons Chickpea Sesame Pâté on (p.
174)
(4) rye crackers with
Sliced celery, jicama, turnips, and green
peppers

Dinner 4 ounces roasted Cornish game hen
(½ cup) wild rice and mushroom stuffing
Steamed asparagus with lemon
Lettuce and sliced water chestnuts with
*1 tablespoon Safflower Dressing with Pa-
paya and Tarragon (p. 169)

Week One—Sunday

Breakfast 1 medium sliced peach
(1 cup) puffed corn and
4 ounces nonfat milk

Lunch *Spinach Fritatta (p. 188)
(½ cup) cooked millet topped with
*1 tablespoon Peanut Dressing with Ginger
and Garlic (p. 170)

Dinner *Five Spice Chicken and Vegetable Stir Sauté
(p. 185)
Leafy green salad with
*1 tablespoon Hazelnut Dressing (p. 169)

Week Two—Monday

Breakfast ½ cup pineapple chunks with
½ cup nonfat cottage cheese
4 ounces nonfat milk

Lunch *(1 cup) Greek Lentil Soup (p. 177)
Endive and bermuda onion salad with
*1 tablespoon French Olive Oil Dressing
(p. 170)
(1 slice) whole-wheat toast

Dinner *4 ounces Baked Salmon in Wine with Savory (p. 185)
*Fresh Tomato Piquant
Green beans almondine
*Coleslaw with Anise, Caraway, and Poppy
Seeds mixed with (p. 194)
*1 tablespoon Safflower Dressing with Papaya and Tarragon (p. 169)

Week Two—Tuesday

Breakfast 2 tablespoons unsweetened raspberry preserves with
4 ounces nonfat yogurt

Lunch 2 hard-cooked eggs on raw spinach with
Celery, artichoke hearts, and roasted red
peppers
*1 tablespoon Walnut Raspberry Vinaigrette
(p. 170)

Dinner 4 ounces broiled lamb patty with ⅛ teaspoon dried mint
(¼ cup) sweet potato
Swiss chard sautéed in
*1 tablespoon French Olive Oil Dressing
(p. 170)

Week Two—Wednesday

Breakfast   1 dried fig chopped in
             (½ cup) oatmeal and
             4 ounces nonfat milk

Lunch   *(1 cup) Vegetable Bean Soup with Oregano
             and Basil (p. 179)
             ½ cup fresh goat cheese on radicchio
             *1 tablespoon Sesame Lemon Dressing
             (p. 171)

Dinner   4 ounces veal strips
             *Ratatouille (p. 192)
             (½ cup) acorn squash

Week Two—Thursday

Breakfast   ½ cup blueberries in
             (2) buckwheat pancakes
             4 ounces nonfat milk

Lunch   *Gazpacho or vegetable soup (p. 177)
             (½ cup) grated raw beets and daikon with
             2 ounces cubed tofu with
             *1 tablespoon Hazelnut Dressing (p. 169)

Dinner   *Eskimo Salad Niçoise (p. 184)
             Steamed broccoli

Week Two—Friday

Breakfast   1 small chopped apple in
             (½ cup) cooked oat bran
             4 ounces nonfat milk

Lunch   *(1 cup) Split Pea and Yam Soup (p. 178)
             Spinach salad with 2 sliced hard-cooked
             eggs
             *1 tablespoon Safflower Dressing with Pa-
             paya and Tarragon (p. 169)

Dinner   *4 ounces Cajun Cod (p. 180)
             Okra and zucchini sautéed in

*1 tablespoon French Olive Oil Dressing
(p. 170)
Cucumber spears

Week Two—Saturday

Breakfast   ½ cup unsweetened cranberry juice
(1 slice) whole-grain toast with
1 tablespoon sesame butter
4 ounces nonfat milk

Lunch   *6 tablespoons Jack's Party Pâté on (p. 174)
(2) rice cakes with
Celery, jicama, and carrot sticks

Dinner   4 ounces flank steak with
*Horseradish Sauce with Dill (p. 173)
Steamed peas, onions, and green beans
Bean sprouts, bamboo shoots, and red peppers stir-sautéed in
*1 tablespoon Peanut Dressing with Ginger
and Garlic (p. 170)

Week Two—Sunday

Breakfast   ½ cup blueberries with
(½ cup) Wheatena
4 ounces nonfat milk

Lunch   *(1 cup) Sherried Black Bean Soup (p. 176)
½ cup feta cheese crumbled in
Green leafy salad with
*1 tablespoon French Olive Oil Dressing
(p. 170)

Dinner   *4 ounces Halibut Shrimp Kabob marinated
in Galliano, Garlic, and Chili (p. 187)
Red and green cabbage with
¼ teaspoon poppyseed stir-sautéed in
*1 tablespoon Peanut Dressing with Ginger
and Garlic (p. 170)

Week Three—Monday

Breakfast   2 tablespoons unsweetened blackberry fruit
preserves on
½ cup nonfat cottage cheese
*(2) Magic Muffins (p. 196)

Lunch   *6 tablespoons Sweetheart Pâté with (p. 175)
Sliced raw mushrooms, cauliflower, and
broccoli
Steamed artichoke dipped in
*1 tablespoon Sesame Lemon Dressing
(p. 171)

Dinner   4 ounces veal strips cooked in white wine
Brussels sprouts
(3½ ounces sliced) Jerusalem artichokes
(sunchokes) topped with
*1 tablespoon Safflower Dressing with Pa-
paya and Tarragon (p. 169)

Week Three—Tuesday

Breakfast   2 tablespoons raisins with
(½ cup) cooked barley or barley flakes
4 ounces nonfat milk

Lunch   Vegetable broth
3 ounces shredded crab in small avocado
with juice of ½ lemon
Sweet onion and celery salad

Dinner   4 ounces broiled chicken with lime juice
(1 small) corn on the cob
Leeks and zucchini stir-sautéed in
*1 tablespoon French Olive Oil Dressing
(p. 170)

Week Three—Wednesday

Breakfast   2 medium dried prunes chopped in
(½ cup) cream of rye
4 ounces nonfat milk

Lunch   *4 ounces Grilled Tuna (p. 186)
           *Chili Mayonnaise (p. 172)
           Warm asparagus
           Spinach and pimento salad with rice vinegar

Dinner   *Old-Fashioned Brisket of Beef with Vegeta-
              bles and Gravy (p. 183)
           Sliced tomatoes with
           *1 tablespoon Hazelnut Dressing (p. 169)

Week Three—Thursday

Breakfast ½ banana
           (½ cup) buckwheat groats (kasha) and
           4 ounces nonfat milk

Lunch   4 ounces sardines with
           Chopped tomato, parsley, and scallions in
           *1 tablespoon Walnut Raspberry Vinaigrette
              (p. 170)
           Baked cauliflower with lemon juice

Dinner   *4 ounces Mediterranean Meatballs with
              (p. 181)
           Spaghetti squash
           Green beans with
           ½ teaspoon toasted sesame seeds
           (1 small) corn on the cob with
           *1 tablespoon Sesame Lemon Dressing
              (p. 171)

Week Three—Friday

Breakfast 2 tablespoons apple butter with
           (½ cup) oatmeal and
           4 ounces nonfat milk

Lunch   *3 Salmon Croquettes with (p. 181)
           *Herbed Hollandaise (p. 172)
           Grated daikon, carrot, and onion salad
           *1 tablespoon Safflower Dressing with Pa-
              paya and Tarragon (p. 169)

Dinner   *1 Stuffed Pepper Oreganato (p. 182)
          Swiss chard sautéed in
          *1 tablespoon Peanut Dressing with Ginger
             and Garlic (p. 170)
          (½ cup) succotash

Week Three—Saturday

Breakfast 1 small sliced peach with
           (1 cup) puffed corn and
           4 ounces nonfat milk

Lunch   4 ounces tuna with
           Juice of ½ lemon
           (2) rice cakes
           *Coleslaw with Anise, Caraway, and Poppy
              Seeds (p. 194)
           *1 tablespoon Safflower Dressing with Pa-
              paya and Tarragon (p. 169)

Dinner   4 ounces shrimp sautéed in white wine and
              parsley
           Steamed yellow squash
           *Ratatouille (p. 192)

Week Three—Sunday

Breakfast ¾ cup strawberries
           *Laced Artichoke Omelet (p. 187)
           (1 slice) rye toast
           4 ounces nonfat milk

Lunch   4 ounces lean broiled turkey burger with
              ⅛ teaspoon fennel
           Steamed green beans
           Chopped parsley, onion, and tomato salad
           *1 tablespoon French Olive Oil Dressing
              (p. 170

Dinner   *4 ounces Lemon Baked Halibut with (p. 182)
           *Garlic Roasted Peppers and Anchovies
              (p. 193)

(¼ cup) yams
Grated jicama on romaine lettuce with champagne vinegar

Recipes

SALAD DRESSINGS AND SAUCES

Hazelnut Dressing

Nut oils are so highly flavored that they make truly
memorable salad dressings. A little bit of oil goes a long
way in flavor.

Serves 8 (1 tablespoon = 1 serving)

> ½ cup hazelnut oil
> 2 tablespoons balsamic vinegar or cider
> vinegar
> ½ teaspoon salt (optional)
> ⅛–¼ teaspoon freshly ground black pepper

Place all ingredients in a small covered jar. Shake well.
Refrigerate.

Safflower Dressing with Papaya and Tarragon

Safflower oil is the lightest and most mildly flavored oil
of all. It is also the most commonly used in diets because it is the highest in cis-linoleic acid, which can
convert into fat-burning GLA. This dressing goes well
with salads and fish.

Serves 9 (1 tablespoon = 1 serving)

> ½ cup safflower oil
> 1 tablespoon papaya juice concentrate
> 1 tablespoon finely chopped sweet onion
> ½ teaspoon tarragon
> ¼ teaspoon salt (optional)

Place all ingredients in a small covered jar. Shake well. Refrigerate.

Walnut Raspberry Vinaigrette

Another nut oil winner, walnut oil lends itself nicely to exotic vinegar accompaniments.

Serves 8 (1 tablespoon = 1 serving)

    ½ cup walnut oil
    2 tablespoons raspberry vinegar
    ½ teaspoon salt (optional)
    ⅛–¼ teaspoon freshly ground black pepper

Place all ingredients in a small covered jar. Shake well. Refrigerate.

French Olive Oil Dressing

Whether used as a salad dressing or to sauté, this basic French-style dressing is a favorite.

Serves 8 (1 tablespoon = 1 serving)

    ½ cup extra virgin olive oil
    2 tablespoons fresh lemon juice
    1 teaspoon Dijon mustard
    ¼ teaspoon salt (optional)

Put all ingredients in a small covered jar. Shake vigorously for 30 seconds and refrigerate. Remove from the refrigerator at least 1 hour before serving to liquefy the oil.

Peanut Dressing with
Ginger and Garlic

Like French Olive Oil Dressing, this can also be used for sautéing as well as on salads.

Serves 8 (1 tablespoon = 1 serving)

½ cup peanut oil
1½ tablespoons finely chopped fresh ginger
1 tablespoon chopped parsley
1 garlic clove, minced
¼ teaspoon salt (optional)

Put all ingredients in a small covered jar. Shake well and refrigerate. Remove at least 1 hour before serving to liquefy the oil.

Sesame Lemon Dressing

Sesame oil has a delicate yet distinctive taste that imparts a nutty flavor to all its companion vegetables.

Serves 8 (1 tablespoon = 1 serving)

½ cup light sesame oil
1 tablespoon fresh lemon juice
½ teaspoon grated fresh lemon zest
¼ teaspoon salt (optional)
½ teaspoon dried dill

Combine all ingredients in a small covered jar. Shake well. Refrigerate.

Bombay Curry Sauce

This sauce enhances all fish dishes.

Serves 4 (3 tablespoons = 1 serving)

1 onion, chopped
1 green cooking apple (such as Granny Smith),
    chopped but not peeled
1 tablespoon butter
2 teaspoons curry powder
1 tablespoon arrowroot
½ cup nonfat milk
½ teaspoon salt (optional)

Sauté onion and apple in butter until tender. Add curry powder and simmer 2 minutes, stirring frequently. Add arrowroot. Mix thoroughly. Add milk and salt (optional), stirring constantly until mixture starts to bubble. Remove from heat.

Fresh Tomato Piquant

This topping adds a refreshing accent to fish and baked potatoes.

Serves 4 (1 heaping tablespoon = 1 serving, but can be eaten in unlimited amounts)

> 4 tablespoons chopped cilantro
> ½ green pepper, chopped
> 1 ripe tomato, seeded and chopped
> 3 tablespoons finely chopped sweet onion
> ½ teaspoon salt (optional)

Combine all ingredients and toss lightly.

Chili Mayonnaise

A homemade real mayonnaise that is perfect with fish.

Makes about 1¼ cups (1 tablespoon = 1 serving)

> 3 egg yolks
> ¼ teaspoon salt (optional)
> 3 tablespoons fresh lemon juice
> 1 cup virgin olive oil
> 1 teaspoon chili powder

Combine the egg yolks, salt, and lemon juice, whisking constantly. Add in the oil slowly until the consistency is smooth. Stir in chili powder. Store in the refrigerator.

Herbed Hollandaise

This light version of the traditional hollandaise is tasty and more nutritious than the original. It is delicious with mild-flavored fish such as sole and salmon, and highlights all vegetables.

Serves 4 (4 tablespoons = 1 serving)

1½ teaspoons arrowroot
¾ cup water
3 tablespoons fresh lemon juice
½ teaspoon salt (optional)
⅛ teaspoon cayenne pepper
1 whole egg, beaten
1 egg yolk, beaten
2 tablespoons mixed chopped fresh herbs
(parsley, thyme, chervil, tarragon, and
basil)

Dissolve arrowroot in water in saucepan. Bring to a boil and cook 1 minute. Reduce heat. Add lemon juice, salt (optional), and cayenne. Combine whole egg with the yolk. Pour mixture into beaten eggs, whisking constantly with a wire whisk. Return to saucepan and cook over low heat, stirring constantly. Remove the sauce from the heat and fold in fresh herbs.

Horseradish Sauce with Dill

An interesting alternative to prepared horseradish, this sauce can be spooned over lean beef or used as a dip for crispy fresh vegetables.

Serves 4 (4 tablespoons = 1 serving)

½ cup nonfat yogurt
½ cup nonfat cottage cheese
½ teaspoon powdered horseradish or 2 teaspoons prepared horseradish
½ teaspoon Worcestershire sauce
½ teaspoon snipped fresh dill
¼ teaspoon salt (optional)

Place all ingredients in a blender or food processor. Blend until smooth. Make sure the cottage cheese is liquefied into a sauce consistency.

PÂTÉS

Chickpea Sesame Pâté

Enjoy this pâté with crackers for a quick meal or serve as a Mediterranean hors d'oeuvre for entertaining. Versatile Chickpea Sesame Pâté also makes a delicious sandwich filler.

Serves 4 (6 tablespoons = 1 serving)

    1½ cups cooked or canned garbanzos
        (chickpeas), drained, reserving liquid
    3 tablespoons chopped onion
    3 tablespoons chopped parsley
    1 large garlic clove, minced
    1 teaspoon dried basil
    ½ teaspoon dried oregano
    ¼ teaspoon ground cumin
    1 tablespoon sesame seed butter
    ¼ cup sesame seeds
    ¼ teaspoon salt (optional)
    2 tablespoons fresh lemon juice
    1 tablespoon liquid from chickpeas

Place all ingredients in food processor or blender. Blend well. Add more liquid if needed when using a blender. Pâté should be thick enough to spread.

Jack's Party Pâté

This is a unique dip, with mysterious ingredients that will leave everyone guessing. (Omit anchovies if on a sodium-restricted diet.)

Serves 8 (6 tablespoons = 1 serving)

    2 13-ounce cans water-packed tuna, rinsed,
        drained, reserving liquid for blender
    1 8-ounce can oysters, rinsed and drained
    1 2-ounce can anchovy fillets, well rinsed and
        drained
    1 garlic clove, minced
    2 tablespoons chopped parsley
    ¼ teaspoon dried dill
    ½ teaspoon Dijon mustard
    ¼ teaspoon dried horseradish or 1 teaspoon
        prepared horseradish
    1 teaspoon fresh lemon juice
    1 teaspoon Bakon Yeast (a brand name yeast
        available in health food stores)

Place all ingredients in food processor or blender and
blend until smooth. Add more liquid if needed when
using a blender.

Sweetheart Pâté

With crackers or raw vegetables, this pâté is also good
for company.

Serves 4 (6 tablespoons = 1 serving)

    1 15½-ounce can salmon, bones and skin
        removed, rinsed but not drained, reserv-
        ing liquid
    2 tablespoons fresh lemon juice
    1 teaspoon dried dill or 1 tablespoon fresh
        dill
    1 tablespoon agar-agar (seaweed gelatin)*
    2 tablespoons salmon liquid
    ½ cup chopped sweet onion
    ¼ cup chopped fresh parsley
    1 tablespoon capers, rinsed and drained

Place salmon, lemon juice and dill in food processor or
blender. Blend for 10 seconds. Dissolve agar-agar in

*Agar-agar is available at health food stores.

salmon liquid in a saucepan and bring to boil. Add dissolved agar-agar to salmon mixture. Stir in onion, parsley, and capers.

SOUPS

In any climate, and any season, soups are satisfying liquid meals. Whether hot or cold they provide good nutrition and round out any dietary plan. Basic stocks from chicken, fish, and vegetables can be used to enhance nutritional value when cooking main dishes, vegetables, and/or grains.

Sherried Black Bean Soup

An exotic variation of a traditional staple.

Serves 4 (1 cup = 1 serving)

> 1 cup dried black beans, washed and soaked
>> in 4 cups water overnight, then drained
> 4 cups water
> 1 tablespoon olive oil
> 2 tablespoons fresh lemon juice
> 1 onion, chopped
> 1 carrot, chopped
> 1 celery stalk with leaves, chopped
> 1 garlic clove, minced
> 2 tablespoons chopped fresh parsley
> 1/8 teaspoon cayenne
> 3/4 teaspoon salt (optional)
> 4 tablespoons sherry
> 1 thinly sliced lemon for garnish
> 1 hard-cooked chopped egg for garnish

Place drained beans in covered pot. Add 4 cups water. Bring to boil and simmer. Add olive oil and lemon juice. Cook 2 to 3 hours until beans are tender. Add onion, carrot, celery, garlic, parsley, cayenne, salt (optional), and sherry. Simmer an additional 30 to 45 minutes until vegetables are tender. Garnish each bowl of soup with lemon slice and chopped egg.

Greek Lentil Soup

The unusual spices give this soup a Mediterranean taste.

Serves 4 (1 cup = 1 serving)

> 1 cup lentils, washed and soaked in 4 cups
>   water overnight
> 3 cups water
> 1 tablespoon olive oil
> 1 tablespoon fresh lemon juice
> 1 onion, chopped
> 1 carrot, chopped
> ½ cup chopped green pepper
> 1 celery stalk with leaves, chopped
> 1 garlic clove, minced
> 2 tablespoons chopped fresh parsley
> ½ bay leaf
> ¾ teaspoon salt (optional)
> ½ teaspoon mustard seed
> ½ teaspoon ground cumin
> 2 tablespoons finely chopped green onions
>   for garnish

Place drained lentils in 3 cups water in covered pot. Bring to boil and simmer. Add olive oil and lemon juice. Cook 30 minutes until lentils are tender. Add onion, carrot, green pepper, celery, garlic, parsley, bay leaf, salt (optional), mustard seed, and cumin. Simmer covered an additional 20 to 30 minutes until vegetables are tender.

Gazpacho

A Spanish cold-soup favorite from south of the border for hot weather. Use garden-fresh ingredients for best flavor.

Serves 4 (1 cup = 1 serving)

  4 tomatoes, peeled, seeded, and coarsely
      chopped
  ½ cup chopped sweet onion
  ½ cucumber, peeled, seeded, and chopped
  ½ green pepper, seeded and chopped
  1 garlic clove, minced
  2 tablespoons olive oil
  3 tablespoons red wine vinegar
  ½ cup ice water
  ½ teaspoon salt (optional)
  2 tablespoons chopped fresh basil or fresh
      parsley

Place all ingredients in a food processor or blender.
Blend until smooth. Serve in chilled bowls.

Split Pea and Yam Soup

The addition of a yam or sweet potato gives a distinc-
tively sweet flavor to this tasty split pea soup.

Serves 4 (1 cup = 1 serving)

  1 cup split peas, washed and soaked in 4
      cups water overnight
  3 cups water
  1 tablespoon olive oil
  1 onion, chopped
  1 carrot, chopped
  1 celery stalk with leaves, chopped
  1 small yam or sweet potato, peeled and
      cubed
  1 garlic clove, minced
  2 tablespoons chopped fresh parsley
  ½ bay leaf
  ¾ teaspoon salt (optional)
  ¼ teaspoon caraway seeds

Place drained split peas and 3 cups water in covered
pot. Bring to boil and simmer. Add olive oil. Cook 30
minutes until split peas are soft. Add onion, carrot,

celery, yam (or sweet potato), garlic, parsley, bay leaf, salt (optional) and caraway seeds. Simmer an additional 20 to 30 minutes until vegetables are tender.

Vegetable Bean Soup with Oregano and Basil

A good basic soup!

Serves 4 (1 cup = 1 serving)

    1 cup dried white beans, washed, sorted,
        and soaked in 4 cups water overnight
    4 cups water
    1 tablespoon olive oil
    1 tablespoon fresh lemon juice
    1 onion, chopped
    1 carrot, chopped
    1 celery stalk with leaves, chopped
    1 garlic clove, chopped
    1 tablespoon chopped fresh parsley
    ½ bay leaf
    ¾ teaspoon salt (optional)
    ½ teaspoon dried oregano
    ¼ teaspoon dried basil

Place drained beans in covered pot. Add 4 cups water. Bring to boil and simmer. Add olive oil and lemon juice. Cook 2 to 3 hours until beans are tender. Add onion, carrot, celery, garlic, parsley, bay leaf, salt (optional), oregano, and basil. Simmer an additional 30 to 45 minutes until vegetables are tender.

MAIN EVENTS

The oil portion in these recipes is controlled for those who are following the 21-Day Master Menu Plan. If you're not using the Master Menus, additional oil can be used—1 tablespoon per person per meal—to add flavor and tenderness to any of the Main Events. **Add** the oil after cooking unless it is olive, canola or peanut oil, which can be used in cooking or for sautéing.

Cajun Cod

A spicy twist for a mild-mannered fish!

Serves 4 (4 ounces cooked fish = 1 serving)

> 1 medium onion, chopped
> 1 green pepper, chopped
> 1 garlic clove, minced
> 1 teaspoon butter
> 2 fresh tomatoes, seeded and chopped
> ½ cup red wine
> ¼ teaspoon thyme
> ½ teaspoon cayenne pepper
> 4 5-ounce cod fillets
> 2 tablespoons fresh lemon juice

Sauté onion, green pepper, and garlic in butter until tender. Add tomatoes, wine, thyme, and cayenne. Bring to a boil. Add cod, reduce heat, cover, and simmer about 10 minutes or until fish flakes. Add lemon juice just before serving.

Chicken with Sherry Dijon

Easy and elegant, this tasty main dish can be served with minimum effort.

Serves 4 (4 ounces cooked chicken = 1 serving)

> 2 whole chicken breasts (2 pounds chicken),
>   skinned and halved
> ½ cup Dijon mustard
> 4 tablespoons sherry

Preheat oven to 350°. Rub chicken breasts with ¼ cup mustard. Place chicken in covered baking pan. Add sherry to remaining ¼ cup mustard for basting. Bake chicken 45 minutes, basting frequently with the Sherry Dijon.

Mediterranean Meatballs

The combination of meatballs with spaghetti squash provides an interesting alternative to the traditional pasta dish, without the pasta!

Serves 4 (4 meatballs = 1 serving)

> 1 pound lean ground round
> ⅓ cup oat bran
> 1 egg, beaten
> ½ teaspoon salt (optional)
> 1 tablespoon chopped fresh parsley
> ½ teaspoon ground cumin
> ⅛ teaspoon ground allspice
> ⅛ teaspoon cayenne
> 1 15-ounce can chicken broth (Health Valley preferred)
> 4 tablespoons instant potatoes (Barbara's preferred)

Preheat broiler. In mixing bowl, combine ground meat, oat bran, egg, salt (optional), parsley, cumin, allspice, and cayenne. Form into 16 balls. Broil 14 inches from heat for 8 minutes. Turn and broil another 4 minutes.

Heat chicken broth and thicken with instant potatoes to make a sauce. Season to taste. Add meatballs to sauce and serve over spaghetti squash.

Salmon Croquettes

A quick way to get your Omega-3s. Herbed Hollandaise is the sauce of choice.

Serves 4 (3 croquettes = 1 serving)

> 1 15½-ounce can salmon, drained, bones and skin removed, and flaked
> ¼ cup crushed cornflakes (salt- and sugar-free)
> ⅓ cup finely chopped onion
> ⅓ cup finely chopped fresh parsley
> 2 tablespoons fresh lemon juice
> 1 egg, beaten
> ⅓ cup crushed cornflakes
> 4 lemon wedges for garnish

Preheat oven to 350°. Combine salmon with ¼ cup crushed cornflakes, onion, parsley, lemon juice, and beaten egg. Shape into 12 croquettes. Roll in the ⅓ cup crushed cornflakes. Bake for 20 to 30 minutes. Serve with lemon wedge garnish.

Stuffed Peppers Oreganato

A healthy touch of bran for an old favorite. You can literally feel your oats!

Serves 4 (1 stuffed pepper = 1 serving)

> 1 pound ground round beef
> ½ onion, finely chopped
> ⅓ cup oat bran
> ½ teaspoon salt (optional)
> ½ teaspoon dried oregano
> ¼ teaspoon paprika
> 5 drops Tabasco
> ⅛ teaspoon cayenne
> 2 large green bell peppers, halved, seeds and
>   membranes removed
> ½ cup chicken broth

Preheat oven to 350°. Mix ground round, onion, and oat bran. Add salt (optional), oregano, paprika, Tabasco, and cayenne. Fill pepper halves with this mixture. Place stuffed peppers in baking dish with chicken broth and cover. Bake for 45 minutes to 1 hour. Serve with broth spooned over peppers.

Lemon-Baked Halibut

An easy-to-prepare dish in which the delicate fish flavor prevails.

Serves 4 (4 ounces cooked fish = 1 serving)

4 5-ounce halibut fillets
1 tablespoon finely minced garlic
1 tablespoon grated fresh lemon zest
⅛ teaspoon salt (optional)

Preheat oven to 350°. Place fillets in baking dish. Sprinkle with garlic and lemon zest. Lightly salt (optional). Cover and bake for 15 to 20 minutes, or until fish is completely white and flakes.

Old-Fashioned Brisket of Beef Dinner with Vegetables and Gravy

This recipe is an East Coast favorite, perfect for a cold winter's day.

Serves 4.

1 3-pound beef brisket, all visible fat removed
2 cups water
1 large onion, stuck with 3 whole cloves
1 large carrot, cut in chunks
2 celery stalks with leaves, cut in 1-inch pieces
1 bay leaf
3 garlic cloves, peeled and pressed
1 teaspoon salt (optional)
1 teaspoon freshly ground pepper
4 small red potatoes
4 carrots, cut in chunks
4 small whole onions, peeled
4 small turnips, peeled (if available)
1 small head cabbage, quartered
1 teaspoon powdered horseradish or 4 teaspoons prepared horseradish

In a large kettle, sear beef brisket over medium heat until browned. Pour off fat. Add water, cloved onion, the biggest carrot, celery, bay leaf, garlic, salt (optional), and pepper. Cover, bring to a boil, and simmer 2½ hours. Remove vegetables and bay leaf and reserve for gravy.

Add potatoes and remaining vegetables in order given.

Sprinkle cabbage with powdered horseradish (or spread with prepared horseradish). Cover and simmer an additional 1½ to 2 hours until meat is tender and vegetables are cooked but not soggy.

To prepare gravy; add vegetables and bay leaf set aside earlier and mash them into meat broth. Bring to boil and reduce to desired consistency. Adjust seasonings to taste and remove bay leaf. To serve, slice cooked brisket across the grain in 1-inch slices. Place on large platter and surround with vegetables. Spoon gravy over brisket.

Eskimo Salad Niçoise

This salad is an Omega-3 adaptation of the classic French salad.

Serves 4

> 4 small red potatoes, unpeeled, steamed,
>   cooled, and sliced
> 2 cups fresh green beans, steamed, cooled,
>   and sliced
> 1 small sweet onion, thinly sliced into rings
> 24 French or Niçoise olives, pitted
> 2 tablespoons chopped fresh parsley
> 4 4-ounce cans water-packed sardines, rinsed
>   and drained
> 3 tablespoons fresh lemon juice
> 4 tablespoons of French Olive Oil Dressing
>   (p. 170)
> Red leaf or butter lettuce leaves for serving
> 2 hard-cooked eggs, shelled and quartered
>   into wedges for garnish

Combine potatoes, green beans, onion rings, olives, and parsley in a large salad bowl. Add sardines, sprinkled with lemon juice. Toss lightly with dressing. Arrange salad on lettuce leaves. Place egg wedges around the salad. Serve chilled.

Five Spice Chicken
and Vegetable Sauté

Crisp and brightly colored, this stir-sauté combination is an enjoyable Main Event.

Serves 4 (4 ounces cooked chicken = 1 serving)

- ½ cup chicken broth
- 2 whole chicken breasts (2 pounds chicken), skinned, boned, and cut into ½-inch pieces
- 2 stalks broccoli, lightly steamed and diagonally sliced
- ½ red pepper, sliced
- 2 carrots, lightly steamed and diagonally sliced
- 2 yellow crookneck squash, diagonally sliced (optional)
- ¼ cup sliced onion
- ¼ cup canned water chestnuts, drained and sliced
- 1 tablespoon chopped fresh parsley
- ¼ teaspoon Chinese five spice powder
- 2 cups cooked brown rice

Heat chicken broth in a skillet or wok. Add chicken and cook until tender. Remove chicken from broth and set aside. Add broccoli, red pepper, carrots, squash, onion, and water chestnuts. Stir and cook 2 to 3 minutes. Add parsley, Chinese five spice powder, and rice. Return cooked chicken to mixture. Stir until thoroughly heated.

Baked Salmon in
Wine with Savory

This salmon is particularly good with the Fresh Tomato Piquant.

Serves 4 (4 ounces cooked fish = 1 serving)

- 4 5-ounce salmon fillets
- ½ cup white wine or vermouth
- ½ teaspoon dried savory leaves
- 4 sprigs cilantro or parsley for garnish

Preheat oven to 350°. Place salmon in baking dish with wine. Sprinkle savory on fish. Cover and bake about 20 minutes, or until fish is completely pink and flakes. Spoon remaining liquid over salmon for more flavor. Garnish with cilantro or parsley.

Spiced Salmon Loaf

Tuna can easily be substituted for salmon in this recipe. You can be creative with your seasonings by adding, for example, a dash of dry mustard, curry powder, or celery seeds in addition to the seasonings already given in the recipe. Dress up your loaf with Bombay Curry Sauce (p. 171).

Serves 4 (4 ounces = 1 serving)

> 1 15½-ounce can salmon, drained, bones
>   and skin removed, and flaked
> ½ cup chopped onion
> ½ cup chopped celery
> 2 tablespoons fresh lemon juice
> 1 teaspoon dried dill
> 1½ teaspoons Worcestershire sauce
> 4 drops Tabasco
> ¼ cup oat bran
> 2 eggs, beaten
> 1 teaspoon butter

Preheat oven to 350°. Combine flaked salmon with onion, celery, lemon juice, and dill in mixing bowl. Add remaining seasonings. Stir in the oat bran. Blend in eggs. Pour into buttered loaf pan and bake for 45 minutes.

Grilled Tuna

Because of tuna's distinct flavor and meaty bite, it is best prepared simply with a zesty sauce. Chili Mayonnaise (p. 172) is a piquant choice.

Serves 4 (4 ounces cooked fish = 1 serving)

4 5-ounce fresh tuna steaks
4 tablespoons white wine

Preheat broiler. Place tuna on baking pan and spoon on wine. Broil about 6 inches from heat until fish is opaque, about 6 minutes. Turn fish over and broil until fish is firm and flakes.

Halibut Shrimp Kabob
Marinated
in Galliano, Garlic and Chili

Company fare. Marinate these kabobs overnight in the refrigerator for fullest flavor.

Serves 4 (4 ounces cooked seafood = 1 serving)

1 pound halibut, cut in 1-inch cubes
8 medium shrimp, peeled and rinsed
2 medium zucchini, cut in ½-inch slices
1 onion, cut in 1-inch cubes
2 tablespoons Galliano wine
1 clove garlic, minced
Juice of 1 lemon
1 tablespoon grated fresh lemon zest
⅛ teaspoon salt (optional)
½ teaspoon chili powder

4 large (or 8 small) bamboo skewers

Thread halibut and shrimp onto skewers, alternating with zucchini and onion cubes. In a bowl, mix Galliano wine, garlic, lemon juice, lemon zest, salt, and chili powder. Marinate for at least 1 hour in refrigerator. Brush skewers with marinade and broil 4 inches away from the heat until cooked on all sides, about 15 minutes.

Laced Artichoke Omelet

Another breakfast or brunch favorite. The wine gives a heady flavor that spikes any appetite.

Serves 4

    2 large cooked artichokes, leaves scraped,
        bottoms coarsely chopped
    1 teaspoon butter
    8 eggs, beaten
    4 tablespoons water
    8 teaspoons white wine
    ½ teaspoon oregano
    ¼ teaspoon salt (optional)
    ⅛ teaspoon pepper

Sauté artichoke pieces in butter until lightly browned.
Mix eggs with water, wine, oregano, salt, and pepper.
Add to artichokes and cook over medium heat until
eggs are set.

Spinach Fritatta

Ideal for breakfast or brunch.

Serves 4

    6 eggs, beaten
    ½ cup nonfat cottage cheese
    1½ cups fresh or frozen spinach, chopped
        and firmly packed
    2 scallions, thinly sliced
    1 teaspoon dried basil or 2 tablespoons fresh
        basil
    ¼ teaspoon salt (optional)
    ⅛ teaspoon grated nutmeg
    1 teaspoon butter

Preheat oven to 350°. Combine eggs, cottage cheese,
spinach, scallions, and seasonings. Melt butter in large
skillet. Add egg mixture and cook over medium heat for
3 minutes. Place in oven and bake an additional 10
minutes or until set.

Vegetables

When freshly crisped for salad or lightly sautéed as a side dish, vegetables are full of natural flavor and texture. They are good fiber sources that can lower cholesterol and protect against colon cancer. Leafy greens and deep yellow vegetables are rich in vitamins A and C and also provide important minerals such as magnesium, potassium, and iron. From tangy Swiss chard to velvety sweet butternut squash, vegetables are taking on a new style. Edible blossoms such as nasturtiums and petite rose petals—unsprayed, of course—are turning up on gourmet salad plates. You can make any vegetable a specialty item by adorning it with a special dressing, sprinkling on fresh herbs, or adding your favorite sauce.

We are surrounded with increasingly exotic vegetables in even the most ordinary supermarkets. The wider variety now available means that your menus are limited only by your creativity. You can add brand-new accents to even your most basic dishes. Some of the new favorites are radicchio (Italian red chicory), sugar snap peas, radish sprouts, bok choy (Chinese mustard cabbage), shiitake mushrooms, baby eggplants, fennel, Vidalia and Walla Walla onions (white and sugar sweet), and chayote squash (known as the starchless biblical squash). In salads or soups, steamed, braised, or stir-sautéed, you can enjoy these vegetables in almost infinite ways. As a colorful puree, any vegetable can perk up your menu quite effortlessly and tastefully.

All vegetables are part of the Master Menu Plan. The amounts of the more starchy ones (such as corn, peas, and potatoes) should initially be limited until the fat burner is working at optimum metabolic strength (usually three weeks on the healthful oils). After the three-week period, both starchy vegetables and grains (such as rice and millet) can be increased.

Timetable for Steaming Fresh Vegetables

Vegetables should be steamed in a stainless steel steamer or colander over boiling water in a covered pot. Taste is enhanced when vegetables are still firm and crunchy after the steaming. The following timetable was designed with this in mind.

Vegetable	Steaming Time
Artichokes	
Globe, whole	45 minutes
Jerusalem or sunchokes, whole	7–10 minutes
Asparagus	
Whole	7–12 minutes
Tips	6–10 minutes
Beans	
Lima	20–30 minutes
Green	8–12 minutes
Wax or yellow	8–12 minutes
Beet greens	3–5 minutes
Beets	
Whole	20–25 minutes
¼-inch slices	3–5 minutes
Broccoli	
Stalks, split	8–10 minutes
Brussels sprouts	8–12 minutes
Cabbage	
Green, quartered	5–7 minutes
Green, shredded	3 minutes
Red, shredded	3 minutes
Carrots	
Whole	15–20 minutes
¼-inch slices	8–12 minutes
Cauliflower	
Whole	20–25 minutes
Florets	7–10 minutes

Celery
Whole	8–12 minutes
Diced	3–7 minutes

Chard, Swiss   3–5 minutes

Corn
On cob	5–8 minutes
Kernels	3–5 minutes

Eggplant
Sliced	8–10 minutes

Kale   3–7 minutes

Kohlrabi
Whole	10–15 minutes
Sliced	3–7 minutes

Okra
Whole	10–12 minutes
Sliced	3–6 minutes

Onions, pearl   5–8 minutes

Parsnips
Whole	13–17 minutes
¼-inch slices	7–10 minutes

Peas, green   3–8 minutes

Potatoes, sweet
Whole	20–30 minutes
½-inch slices	7–10 minutes

Potatoes, White
Whole	20–30 minutes
½-inch slices	7–10 minutes

Snow peas (pea pods)   3–5 minutes

Spinach   3–5 minutes

Squash, summer
Whole	15–25 minutes
¼-inch slices	8–10 minutes

Squash, winter	
Whole	20–30 minutes
¼-inch slices	7–10 minutes
Tomatoes	
Whole	5–8 minutes
½-inch slices	3–5 minutes
Turnips	
Whole	12–18 minutes
½-inch slices	3–6 minutes
Zucchini	
Whole	8–12 minutes
¼-inch slices	3–6 minutes

Ratatouille

This is a tasty side dish and makes a wonderful topping for fish, beef, and poultry dishes. Try it on baked potatoes!

Serves 4 (1½ cups = 1 serving)

    4 tablespoons olive oil
    1 onion, coarsely chopped
    1 green bell pepper, seeded, cut into 1-inch
        pieces
    1 eggplant, unpeeled, cut into 1-inch cubes
    2 zucchini, cut into ¼-inch rounds
    3 tomatoes, peeled, seeded, and chopped
    ½ teaspoon salt (optional)
    2 teaspoons chopped fresh basil or ½ tea-
        spoon dried basil
    ½ teaspoon dried oregano
    2 garlic cloves, minced

In a large covered saucepan, sauté onion and green pepper in olive oil until lightly browned. Add eggplant and zucchini. Cook until tender. Add tomatoes, salt (optional), basil, and oregano. Cover and cook over low heat, stirring occasionally, 35 to 40 minutes. Add garlic and cook uncovered for 10 minutes.

Garlic Roasted Peppers and Anchovies

Serve as antipasto, salad, or vegetable. For those on a low-sodium diet, omit the anchovies.

Serves 4 (½ cup = 1 serving)

> 4 large bell peppers, halved, seeds and
>   membranes removed (preferably a com-
>   bination of green, red, and yellow)
> 1 head of garlic
> 1 tablespoon olive oil
> ¼ cup coarsely chopped fresh parsley
> 1 2-ounce can anchovy fillets, well drained
>   and rinsed to remove extra salt

Preheat broiler. Roast peppers on baking sheet under open broiler, turning every few minutes until skin has browned. Remove peppers and put them in a brown paper bag to rest for at least 15 minutes. Peel skin and cut into long thin strips. Dry thoroughly on paper towels.

Separate garlic into cloves and place in boiling water for 15 minutes. Cool and remove skins. Place garlic, olive oil, parsley, and anchovies in a blender. Blend to make a paste. Toss paste with peppers and refrigerate 1 hour or longer before serving.

Minted Carrots and Snow Peas

A pleasing twist to an old favorite.

Serves 4 (½ cup = 1 serving)

> 6 carrots, cut into thin strips
> 1 teaspoon butter
> ¼ pound snow peas (Chinese pea pods),
>   strings removed from both sides
> 1 teaspoon chopped fresh mint

Sauté carrots in butter 7 to 10 minutes. Add snow peas and cook an additional 1 to 2 minutes. Remove from heat. Stir in mint and serve.

Coleslaw with Anise, Caraway, and Poppy Seeds

A delicious coleslaw without mayonnaise.

Serves 4 (1 cup = 1 serving)

    1 small head green cabbage, shredded
    2 carrots, grated
    ½ cup nonfat plain yogurt
    ¼ teaspoon anise seeds
    ¼ teaspoon poppy seeds
    ¼ teaspoon caraway seeds
    ¼ teaspoon dry mustard
    2 tablespoons fresh lemon juice

Place cabbage and carrots in mixing bowl. Combine yogurt, all the seeds, mustard, and lemon juice. Toss cabbage and carrots with yogurt mixture to cover thoroughly. Serve chilled.

SWEET DELIGHTS

New and exotic varieties of fruit are finding their way into mainstream markets, along with their vegetable cousins. Fiber-packed fruits are high in vitamins and minerals but low in sodium. They can be enjoyed as hot or cold cereal toppings, whether fresh or dried, and as low-calorie snacks between meals. Vary your fruit intake by enjoying the mildly tart taste of fresh kiwi, or try a plump persimmon cut in half and eaten like a melon. Fresh fruits can be frozen for several hours and then pureed into sugar-free sorbets. Bananas, berries, and peaches are tasty sorbet favorites. Succulent papaya, pineapple, guava, and mango are especially high in digestive enzymes and can help a sensitive digestive tract when eaten fully ripe. Enjoy fruit as the perfect snack all by itself, because its nutritional value is best utilized for digestion when not combined with other foods. This is also true for the fruit-based puddings and gelatins presented in this section.

If you are following the 21 Day Master Menu Plan, remember that Sweet Delights can be enjoyed as one of the 1–3 daily fruit servings after the three-week period.

Baked Apple with Raisins, Cinnamon, and Nutmeg

Baked apples provide a good fruit variation for breakfast or any time of day.

Serves 4 (1 apple = 1 serving)

> 4 cooking apples, such as MacIntosh or
>   Granny Smith, cored and pared
> 1 tablespoon unsweetened apple juice
> 2 tablespoons loose raisins
> 1 teaspoon ground cinnamon
> ¼ teaspoon grated nutmeg

Preheat oven to 350°. Place apples and apple juice in baking dish. Fill centers with mixture of raisins, cinnamon, and nutmeg. Cover and bake for 45 minutes.

Vanilla Pears

Fresh peaches, plums, or nectarines can be substituted for pears when in season.

Serves 4 (2 pear halves = 1 serving)

> 4 pears, cored, peeled, and halved
> 1 tablespoon water
> 1 teaspoon allspice
> 12 drops vanilla extract

Preheat oven to 325°. Place pears and water in baking dish. Sprinkle with allspice and drizzle each pear half with 3 drops of vanilla extract. Cover and bake for about 20 minutes.

Old-Fashioned Applesauce

This is delicious served warm or chilled.

Serves 4 (½ cup = 1 serving)

  4 cooking apples, peeled, cored, and chopped
  2 tablespoons unsweetened apple juice
  2 tablespoons honey
  ¼ teaspoon ground cinnamon
  ⅛ teaspoon grated nutmeg

In a saucepan, cook apples in apple juice over low to medium heat about 12 to 15 minutes. Cool slightly. Place in blender with honey, cinnamon, and nutmeg. Blend until smooth.

Rhubarb Sauce

Rhubarb, like applesauce, is good warm or chilled.

Serves 4 (½ cup = 1 serving)

  1 pound rhubarb, chopped
  1 tablespoon water
  4 tablespoons honey
  ½ teaspoon cinnamon

In a saucepan, cook rhubarb in water over low to medium heat 10 to 15 minutes. Blend in honey and cinnamon.

The Magic Muffin

This muffin represents dietary magic because the oat bran component is a powerful cholesterol tamer.

Serves 8 (1 muffin = 1 serving)

2 teaspoons butter
1 cup + 2 tablespoons oat bran
1½ teaspoons baking powder
1 teaspoon ground cinnamon
¼ teaspoon salt (optional)
1 tablespoon chopped almonds
¼ cup + 2 tablespoons nonfat milk
1 egg, beaten
2 tablespoons honey
1 apple, cored and chopped

Preheat oven to 425°. Butter 8 muffin cups. Mix oat bran, baking powder, cinnamon, and salt (optional) in a bowl. Stir in almonds. In a separate bowl combine milk, egg, honey, and chopped apple. Make a well in dry ingredients and add milk mixture. Stir just until moistened. Spoon into prepared muffin cups. Bake for 15 minutes.

NOUVELLE PUDDINGS

Coconut Rum Pudding

Nutritious and delicious.

Serves 4 (½ cup = 1 serving)

2 cups nonfat milk
⅛ teaspoon salt (optional)
3 tablespoons arrowroot
4 tablespoons honey
1 egg, beaten
½ teaspoon coconut extract
½ teaspoon rum extract

In a saucepan, heat 1½ cups milk and salt (optional) at low to medium heat. Dissolve arrowroot in remaining ½ cup milk. Add arrowroot and milk to already heated milk and bring to gentle boil, stirring constantly as nonfat milk scorches easily. Reduce heat, add honey, and mix thoroughly. Add 1 cup of hot pudding mixture to egg in mixing bowl, stirring enough to heat egg but not cook it. Return to saucepan, stirring constantly to thoroughly mix all ingredients. Return to boil, still stirring constantly. Remove from heat. Add flavor extracts. Cool 20 minutes before refrigeration. Serve chilled.

Maple Pudding

An easy variation on the pudding theme.

Serves 4 (½ cup = 1 serving)

Follow recipe for Coconut Rum Pudding. Substitute 5 tablespoons maple syrup and ½ teaspoon pure maple flavoring for the coconut and rum extracts.

Fruit Compote Pudding

Another healthful variation to please a sweet tooth.

Serves 4 (½ cup = 1 serving)

Follow recipe for Coconut Rum Pudding. Mix ½ cup mixed sun-dried fruit (figs, dates, apricots) into pudding after removing from heat.

Tapioca Pudding

Who doesn't like tapioca pudding?

Serves 4 (½ cup = 1 serving)

> 3 tablespoons granulated tapioca
> 1½ cups nonfat milk
> ⅛ teaspoon salt (optional)
> 3 tablespoons honey
> 1 egg, beaten
> 1 teaspoon vanilla extract

In a saucepan, heat tapioca, milk, and salt (optional) over low heat. Bring to a slow boil and cook uncovered for 5 minutes, stirring frequently. Reduce heat. Add honey and blend thoroughly. Pour some of the hot mixture into the egg in a mixing bowl, stirring enough to heat egg but not cook it. Return mixture to saucepan, stirring frequently, and bring to gentle boil. Simmer 3 minutes over low heat. Remove from heat and add vanilla extract. Cool 20 minutes before refrigerating. Serve chilled.

FRUIT GELATINS

Cherry Gelatin

Any unsweetened fruit juice can be used in this basic gelatin recipe. Health food stores carry many unusual combinations of unsweetened fruit juice, such as papaya, apple-boysenberry, and apple-strawberry.

Serves 4 (½ cup = 1 serving)

> 2 cups unsweetened cherry juice
> 2 tablespoons agar-agar

Combine juice and agar-agar in saucepan. Boil for 30 seconds. Cool 20 minutes and refrigerate until set (about 2 hours). Serve chilled.

Piña Colada Gelatin

Serves 4 (½ cup = 1 serving)

Follow recipe for Cherry Gelatin, substituting unsweetened pineapple-coconut juice for cherry juice.

Pomegranate Gelatin

Serves 4 (½ cup = 1 serving)

Follow recipe for Cherry Gelatin, substituting pomegranate juice for cherry juice.

Carob Gelatin

It may not be chocolate pudding, but close enough.

Serves 4 (½ cup = 1 serving)

> ⅔ cup Carob Dream dessert topping (from
>   health food store)
> 1⅓ cups water
> 2 tablespoons agar-agar

Mix all ingredients in a saucepan and boil for 30 seconds. Cool 20 minutes and refrigerate until set (about 2 hours). Serve chilled.

FRESH FRUIT SORBETS

Blueberry Banana

This sorbet stands well on its own as an alternative to ice cream.

Serves 4 (½ cup = 1 serving)

> 1¾ cups blueberries (fresh or frozen)
> 2 bananas, sliced
> 1 tablespoon honey
> ½ teaspoon fresh lemon juice

Place all ingredients in food processor or blender and blend until smooth. Place in plastic container and freeze at least 2 hours. Take out partially frozen fruit and stir well to break up ice crystals. Return to freezer to completely freeze. Let fruit sorbet stand 15 minutes at room temperature before serving.

Ginger Pear Sorbet

A spicy fruit flavor to satisfy your taste buds.

Serves 4 (½ cup = 1 serving)

> 4 pears, peeled, cored, and cubed
> ¼ teaspoon powdered ginger
> 1 tablespoon honey
> ½ teaspoon fresh lemon juice

Place all ingredients in food processor or blender and blend until smooth. Freeze in plastic container for 2 hours. Take out partially frozen fruit and stir well to break up ice crystals. Return to freezer and freeze completely. Let stand at room temperature 15 minutes before serving.

Grain Creations

Whole-grain cereals are naturally high sources of fiber, minerals, and B vitamins. Their high complex-carbohydrate content sustains blood sugar levels because of the slow release of energy. The basic recipe for most grains is easy to remember: 2 cups of grain to 1 cup of water. Millet, barley, and wild rice require 3 cups of water, and corn meal needs 4 cups. The grain is added to the boiling water and simmered over low heat for about 30 to 40 minutes. Low, slow cooking temperatures do not destroy the minerals and vitamins that are vulnerable to the effects of high temperatures.

A tiny grain seed called amaranth is a fairly new addition to store shelves. It was widely used by the Aztecs in Mexico hundreds of years ago and was revered as a magical, mystical grain. Amaranth is one of the highest protein grains and is a good source of lysine, an essential amino acid lacking in all other grains. Amaranth can be used alone as a cereal or added to the batter of breads and baked goods. Added to popcorn, it can also be popped, although the grain does not expand.

Another exotic high-protein grain is quinoa. Reputed to be as high or higher in protein value than amaranth, quinoa is an abundant source of the amino acids methionine and cystine as well as lysine. Known as the "mother grain" of the Incas, quinoa is low in gluten and makes a nutritious substitute for wheat-sensitive individuals.

For cold winter mornings, I suggest either rye or buckwheat groats (or kasha). These hearty cereals are good for the circulation and will keep you warm. In hot

weather you can choose from any of the other varieties
eaten cold, already prepared.

Food Equivalents

Your kitchen is your personal health laboratory. The
following exchange lists are designed for your culinary
creativity. You can substitute, mix, or match the food
choices to fit your needs and tastes. Each food portion
is interchangeable with all others listed in the same
group because, in the portions given, they provide the
same kinds of nutrients.

Brand names are generally not specified in this section. Refer to "Stocking and Storing the Staples" (p. 120)
for preferred brands.

The Essential and Healthy Fats

A combined total of 2 tablespoons can be chosen from
among the following recommended fat equivalents. The
2 tablespoon amount is the daily quantity necessary to
meet nutritional requirements and appetite satisfaction.
The higher amount of essential fatty acids contained in
expeller-pressed safflower, sunflower, corn, and soy especially activate your fat burner to convert calories into
heat rather than store them as fat for effective and
lasting weight loss.

Each food source is broken down to equal the equivalent of 1 tablespoon of oil, so that you have the option
to vary your beneficial fat intake from a number of
delicious sources.

Crude or unrefined oils (expeller-pressed)	1 tablespoon
Avocado	½ small
Nuts (raw or home-toasted)	15 small
Seeds (raw or home-toasted)	1½ teaspoons

| Sesame seed butter | 1 tablespoon |
| Mayonnaise (commercially made from expeller-pressed oil or homemade with expeller-pressed oil) | 1 tablespoon |

Protein

Include a total of 6 to 8 ounces daily from any combination of the following protein sources. Each food source is broken down to equal the equivalent of 1 ounce of fish, poultry, or lean beef. Limit egg intake to 4 to 6 per week. It is best to spread out protein foods throughout the day, dividing them between breakfast, lunch, and dinner.

Cheese	¼ cup
Egg	1
Fish and seafood	
Salmon, halibut, perch, sole:	1 ounce
Oysters, clams, shrimp, scallops:	5 small
Anchovies (well rinsed):	9 fillets
Sardines:	3 medium
Canned Salmon, tuna, crab:	¼ cup
Poultry and beef	
Turkey, chicken, beef, veal, lamb:	1 ounce
Tofu	1 ounce

Vegetables

Include a daily total of 4 or more servings from the list below. Each serving equals ½ cup (4 ounces). Celery, cucumbers, endive, escarole, lettuce, radishes, and assorted sprouts are especially desirable for meal planning and snacking because of their low-calorie content and should be counted as "freebies."

Artichoke (1 small whole)
Bamboo shoots
Beans, green or yellow
Beets
Broccoli
Brussels sprouts
Cabbage
Carrots (1 medium)
Cauliflower
Celery
Chicory
Chilies: green or red
Chinese cabbage
Cucumbers
Eggplant
Endive
Escarole
Greens: beets, chard, kale, collard, dandelion, mustard, spinach, turnip, radicchio, arugula, mache, broccoli rabe
Jicama
Jerusalem artichoke (sunchoke)
Mushrooms
Okra
Onions
Peppers: green or red
Radishes: red or Daikon
Rutabaga
Sauerkraut
Seaweed: nori and kelp
Sprouts: mung bean, adzuki, alfalfa, clover, radish
Squash: summer, spaghetti, chayote
Snow peas
Tomatoes
Tomato juice
Turnips
Vegetable juice cocktail
Water chestnuts (4)
Watercress
Zucchini

Note: Herbs—parsley, cilantro, basil, mint, oregano, rosemary, dill, tarragon, marjoram, etc.—can be used freely.

Fruits

These fruits are the recommended snacks to be enjoyed between meals. Eat a maximum of 3 fruits daily.

Apple	1 small (2-inch diameter)
Apple butter (sugar free)	2 tablespoons
Apple juice or cider	1/3 cup
Applesauce (unsweetened)	1/2 cup
Apricots (fresh)	2 medium
Apricots (dried)	4 halves
Banana	1/2 small
Berries: boysenberries, blackberries, blueberries, raspberries	1/2 cup

Cantaloupe	¼ (6-inch diameter)
Cherries	10 large
Dates	2
Figs (fresh)	1 large
Figs (dried)	1 small
Fruit cocktail (in its juice)	½ cup
Fruit preserves & spreads (sugar free)	2 tablespoons
Grapefruit	½ small
Grapefruit juice	½ cup
Grapes	12
Grape juice	¼ cup
Honeydew melon	⅛ (7-inch diameter)
Mandarin oranges	¾ cup
Kiwi	1 medium
Mango	½ small
Nectarine	1 small
Orange	1 small
Orange juice	½ cup
Papaya	¾ cup
Peach	1 medium
Pear	1 small
Persimmon	1 medium
Pineapple	½ cup
Pineapple juice	⅓ cup
Plums	2 medium
Prunes	2 medium
Prune juice	¼ cup
Raisins	2 tablespoons
Strawberries	¾ cup
Tangerine	1 large
Watermelon	1 cup

Complex Carbohydrates

Include 2 OR MORE SERVINGS from the following variety on a daily basis. This is the group where servings can be added or subtracted, depending upon weight loss needs. Grain selections, particularly gluten-based cereals such as wheat, oats, rye, and barley should be kept to a minimum. The starchy vegetable group should be emphasized.

Starchy Vegetables:

Corn (on the cob)	1 (4" long)
Corn (cooked)	⅓ cup
Parsnips	1 small
Peas (fresh)	¾ cup
Potatoes (sweet, yam)	¼ cup
Potatoes, white (baked or boiled)	1 small
Potatoes, white (mashed)	½ cup
Pumpkin	¾ cup
Rutabaga	1 small
Squash (winter, acorn, butternut)	½ cup

Breads:

Bagel, whole wheat	½ small
Bread rye, pumpernickle, whole wheat	1 slice
Breadsticks	4 (7" long)
Bun hamburger, hot dog	½
Croutons	½ cup
English muffin	½
Pancakes	2 (3" diam.)
Pita bread	½ of 6" pocket
Rice cakes	2
Roll	1 (2" diam.)
Tortilla	1 (6" diam.)

Cereals and Grains:

Barley (cooked)	½ cup
Bran flakes	½ cup
Bran (unprocessed rice or wheat)	⅓ cup
Buckwheat groats (kasha) (cooked)	⅓ cup

Cream of rice (cooked)	½ cup
Grapenuts	¼ cup
Grits (cooked)	½ cup
Millet (cooked)	½ cup
Oatmeal	½ cup
Popcorn	3 cups
Puffed rice, wheat, millet & oats	1½ cups
Rice (brown, cooked)	⅓ cup
Rice (wild, cooked)	½ cup
Shredded wheat biscuit	1 large
Wheatena (cooked)	½ cup
Wheat germ	1 oz. or 3 Tbsp.

Crackers:

Matzoh, whole wheat	½ (6″ × 4″)
Pretzels, whole grain	1 large
Rice Wafers, brown rice (Westbrae)	4
Rye crispbread crackers (Wasa)	1½ crackers
Wheat crackers, whole wheat (Ak-Mak)	4 crackers
(Health Valley)	13 crackers

Flours:

Arrowroot	2 Tbsp
Buckwheat	3 Tbsp
Cornmeal	3 Tbsp
Cornstarch	2 Tbsp
Potato flour	2½ Tbsp
Rice flour	3 Tbsp
Soya powder	3 Tbsp
Whole wheat	3 Tbsp

Legumes:

Beans, dried (cooked) lima, soy, navy, pinto, kidney, garbanzos, black	½ cup
Beans, baked plain	½ cup
Lentils, dried (cooked)	½ cup

| Peas, dried (cooked) | ½ cup |

Pasta

Noodles, macaroni, spaghetti (cooked)	½ cup
Noodles, rice (cooked)	½ cup
Noodles, whole wheat (cooked)	½ cup
Pasta, whole wheat (cooked)	½ cup

Dairy (optional)

The daily intake of 2 servings of cow's milk, nonfat dairy products, or goat's milk products from the following alternatives is up to you. Remember, the label should read "0 grams fat" to qualify as a healthy fat cow's milk dairy product. Many who cannot tolerate cow's milk do well with goat's milk, especially children.

Milk: nonfat cow's milk, goat's milk	1 cup
Yogurt: nonfat cow's milk, plain; goat's milk yogurt, plain	1 cup
	1 cup
Soya powder (substitute for milk)	3 tablespoons

Note: If you can find pasteurized, nonhomogenized cow's milk, you can use it to replace both the nonfat and the goat's milk servings cup for cup. Just pour off the cream and give it to your grateful friends.

Ten Transitional Tips

The following dietary suggestions will assist you in changing to a healthier eating plan:

• One tablespoon of freshly ground flaxseed (kept in fridge or freezer) can be added to cereal right before serving time. It's a great natural laxative for both young and old.

• Use Worcestershire sauce to replace soy sauce. Worcestershire contains 55 mg. of sodium per tablespoon, as compared to 1000 mg. of sodium per tablespoon in soy sauce. The flavor is great with sauces, meatloaf, and even on vegetables.

• To replace cream and whole milk in soups and sauces, substitute arrowroot and/or instant mashed potatoes from health food store.

• Pureed vegetables such as winter squash, broccoli, carrots, sweet potatoes, and green peas are great for side dishes drizzled with a drop of virgin olive oil.

• Ground turkey can replace ground beef in loaves.

• For added fat-fighting fiber, mix 1 tablespoon oat bran in your hot cereal.

• Cranberry sauce is a low sodium, virtually fat-free replacement for heavy gravies on meat, fish, and poultry.

• Grated orange peel or lemon rind with ground nutmeg is a zesty cooking pickup. Add to fish or chicken before broiling and to squash before baking.

• Horseradish (either prepared or powdered) can be added to nonfat yogurt as a quick and easy dip, or sauce for fish and vegetables. The recipe is 1 tablespoon horseradish to 1 cup nonfat yogurt.

• For hard-core hamburger lovers, try 1 teaspoon of Angostura Bitters to 1 pound lean ground beef to substitute for bacon, cheese, and mayonnaise.

17

SPICES AND
HERBS OF LIFE

*The earth yields her seed, her
vegetables, her fruit and her greens;
use as the Creator provided them.*
—ANN WIGMORE, raw foods pioneer.

Folk medicine for centuries touted the healing effects of certain herbs and spices. Herbs are especially rich in the minerals manganese, potassium, and iron. Dill, fennel, mint, and savory are all reputed to aid digestion, while rosemary was prized in Shakespeare's time to be good for the memory, sage tea was considered a strongly medicinal spring tonic, and thyme was revered as a medieval symbol of courage. Bay leaves have always been used to keep bugs out of the cupboard and out of flour, and oil of cloves can relieve a toothache.

Herbal Magic

Many modern medicines have their origins in herbs (such as digitalis from the foxglove plant and aspirin from willow bark). Valium, the most widely prescribed tranquilizer, is based on the herb valerian root. Capsules of powdered ginger are a modernday preventive against motion sickness. Cardamom is revered as an aphrodisiac in the Middle East. The antioxidant properties of rosemary are now being extracted for use as natural food preservatives.

It is the volatile oil in each herb that contains much of the herb's health-enhancing qualities. To release the volatile oil, use a mortar and pestle or a small grinder. To preserve the oil, store in a tightly sealed opaque container in a cool place away from the stove, oven, or dishwasher. You can protect ground herbs and spices from the ravages of heat, air, and light in these ways.

Essential oils can be used instead of dried herbs and spices. They have a longer shelf life than their herb and spice counterparts and blend better with other recipe ingredients. One teaspoon of dried herb or spice is equal to two drops of the essential oil. While there are many oils that can be used safely in cooking, such as peppermint, anise, rosemary, lemon, and lime, not all oils are suitable for consumption.

Seasoning Savvy

Here are some of my flavoring favorites that add spice to your palate without added salt, sugar, or damaged fats. Wines and liqueurs are good flavor boosters because the alcohol and calories are burned off in cooking, while the flavor remains. The flavorful skins of lemons, limes, and oranges (with the white membrane detached) add zing to a number of foods. These "zests," like herbs, spices, wines, and liqueurs, are also piquant cooking essences.

FOOD	FLAVOR FIXER
FISH	Basil, dillweed, ginger, garlic, fennel, chervil, onions, lemon zest, capers, saffron, Pernod, dry sherry
MEAT	
Beef	Thyme, cumin, horseradish, basil, clove, garlic, curry, cardamom, red wine
Lamb	Rosemary, mint, cinnamon, garlic, allspice, curry

Poultry	Tarragon, rosemary, curry, paprika, lemon zest, garlic, mustard, horseradish, sage, thyme, lime zest, vodka, tequila
EGGS	Black pepper, nutmeg, white wine, parsley, chervil
BEANS	Thyme, coriander, sage, garlic, shallots, chives, curry, savory, cumin, turmeric, beer
SOUPS	Bay leaf, dill, parsley, onions, celery seed, sherry

VEGETABLES

Asparagus	Tarragon, parsley, mustard seed, lemon zest
Beets	Dill, cloves, savory, garlic, ginger, bay leaf
Broccoli	Mustard seed, onion, garlic, tarragon
Brussels sprouts	Basil, sage, thyme, garlic, caraway seed
Cabbage	Caraway seed, mint, nutmeg, savory, ginger, gin, allspice
Carrots	Allspice, dill, marjoram, bay leaf, fennel, ginger, Pernod
Cauliflower	Celery seed, mace, caraway seed, tarragon, cumin
Cucumber	Basil, dill, mint
Eggplant	Oregano, marjoram
Greens	Chives, dill, tarragon, basil
Onions	Thyme, nutmeg, oregano, sage
Peas	Rosemary, savory, poppy seed, mint
Potatoes	Chives, bay leaf, thyme, caraway seed
Spinach	Basil, mace, nutmeg, marjoram
Squash	Cloves, fennel, ginger, nutmeg
Sweet potatoes	Cardomom, cinnamon, cloves, allspice
Tomatoes	Basil, celery seed, sesame seed, capers, Pernod, dry Madeira *Note:* Fennel and anise seed give a sausage flavor to tomato sauce

FRUITS

Apples	Allspice, cinnamon, nutmeg, coriander, ginger

Pears	Cardamom, vanilla extract, champagne
Bananas	All wines, brandy, rum
Compote	All wines, brandy, rum
Dried fruit mixtures	Fruit brandies
Grapefruit	Bourbon (*Note:* A drop of olive oil brushed on a grapefruit, then broiled, sweetens it considerably. Bitters are also very good on grapefruit.)

Spice It Up

If you like experimenting with different combinations of flavors, here are some suggestions to get started.

Oriental blends on fish and chicken (ginger, cinnamon, anise, nutmeg, and cloves)

Italian blends on steamed vegetables (oregano, marjoram, thyme, savory, basil, and rosemary)

Indian blends on grains and beans (cumin, dill, allspice, cardamom, and turmeric)

Mexican blends on egg dishes (chili pepper, garlic powder, and cumin)

Pumpkin Pie spice on oatmeal or squash (cinnamon, ginger, allspice, and nutmeg)

Some Like It Hot

Cajun seasonings are now available in seven varieties from Paul Prudhommes's Cajun Magic spices. Call 1-800-654-6017 for the nearest outlet or to order direct.

18

EATING OUT SMART

*Gaining health without maintaining it
is like winning the war but losing the peace.*
—Anonymous

Whether you are on land, in the air, or traveling the high seas, following the New Nutrition Diet can be a satisfying proposition. Fish and fiber-rich foods, like beans, grains, vegetables, salads, and fruit are your mainstays, and these can be found almost everywhere. Food selection outside the home has become fun and convenient due to the popularity of salad bars and the addition of lighter entrees for the calorie conscious in most restaurants across the country.

The golden rule is simple: Order mainly foods containing the essential or healthy fats. Best bets are all kinds of fish and shellfish, grilled, broiled, and poached or baked in wine and seasoned with garlic and onions. Fresh salads, steamed vegetables, corn on the cob, and plain baked potatoes (you can add a dot of butter for flavor) are wise food choices. Ask for fruit for dessert or eat it as a snack between meals. Olive oil is probably the only available healthful fat cooking and salad oil you will be able to order, but go easy with the olive oil, about 1 tablespoon per meal to be exact. You can truly enjoy this taste treat guilt-free because it is a heart-healthy fat choice.

Remember that the undesirable hidden fats, salts, and sugars abound in sauces and dressings. Choose simple dishes and request *all* sauces on the side. In this

way you have more control over flavor and the bad fats.
Side orders of sliced onions or chives are usually available at most restaurants and are an easy source of
flavor. A small dab of butter can add a grateful touch to
otherwise tasteless cooked vegetables.

Remember that tuna, chicken, and egg salad usually
contain too much mayonnaise and so should be avoided
on a daily basis. Actually, mayonnaise is a processed
food, containing heat-treated and partially hydrogenated oil, in the form of partially hydrogenated soybean
oil. Wherever possible, substitute small amounts of mustard or yogurt for mayonnaise.

Where's the Beef?

In standard restaurants when fish is not available or
you feel like a change, turkey, chicken, and lean ground
beef are good alternatives. Yes, lean beef. Eaten in moderation, about twice a week, beef has a respectable
place on the menu. There are several trace minerals
such as copper, iron, zinc, and manganese that red
meat provides and that cannot be found in such high
amounts in other foods. Lean roast beef is a viable
choice. Chef's salads (without the ham), Greek, and
Niçoise are also smart selections.

Oatmeal and poached or soft-, medium-, and hard-
cooked eggs are easily obtainable for breakfast in most
places. A good luncheon or dinner meal might consist
of a hearty soup such as minestrone, lentil, mushroom,
barley, or Manhattan clam chowder. Soups are great
with a salad and a slice of whole-wheat or rye bread.
You can skim off any excess fat in the soup by dropping
in an ice cube and scooping the melted cube off the top
along with the fat, which has been brought to the surface.

Small Plates

In some of the newer restaurants, creative diners can design their own meals by selecting appetizers and salads without main courses. Several fine eateries even offer the entire menu scaled down to appetizer-portion size often called tapas. This trend is a boon to Eating Out Smart because the wide variety of vegetables, light proteins, and salads fits the guidelines set by the New Nutrition Diet.

Ethnic Eating

When Americans eat out, says a Gallup poll taken in 1985, they choose from American-style restaurants (56 percent), followed by Italian (14 percent), Chinese (12 percent), Mexican (8 percent), with French and Japanese last (at 2 percent). In each of these restaurants you can order safely and walk out feeling completely satisfied.

Italian Restaurants

For a change of pace at Italian restaurants, you might enjoy a pasta with pesto sauce (that delightful combination of basil, garlic, and olive oil with pine nuts). This is the place where you can make starch, in the form of pasta or beans, the focus of your meal. Remember your food combinations and do not combine wheat (the pasta dishes) with a meat or clam sauce. Meatless marinara or plain garlic and oil are good alternatives to the pesto sauce. Pasta primavera—pasta with vegetables—is an excellent choice. If pasta is not your thing, then order veal as your main entree. Veal marsala, piccata, and scallopini are delicious with a leafy green salad and sautéed vegetables.

Chinese Restaurants

First specify that your dishes be made without monosodium glutamate (MSG), sugar, salt, and soy sauce. Then inquire about the oil used in cooking. Many Chinese restaurants use peanut oil. If so, you are in luck. If not, then specify no oil along with the other omissions (MSG, sugar, and soy sauce). Assuming that peanut oil is used, choose chicken, shrimp, and flank steak dishes with steamed rice and vegetables, such as snow peas, water chestnuts, onion, broccoli, scallions, bamboo shoots, and Chinese cabbage (bok choy). Stir-fries with sprouts, vegetables, cellophane noodles (rice or mung bean noodles) and small amounts of chicken, beef, tofu, or seafood are tasty choices. Buddha's Delight (a mixed vegetable dish) is always a winner. The fortune—without the cookie—is for dessert.

Mexican Restaurants

In the Mexican restaurants, black bean soup, gazpacho, and small amounts of guacamole laced with lots of fresh lemon or lime juice are tasty selections. Tortillas can be steamed instead of fried, and chili with or without the carne might also please your palate. Chicken with rice or shrimp with rice is a wise entree selection. Do avoid refried beans, which are usually made with lard.

French Restaurants

Choose "nouvelle cuisine," which is much lighter than the traditional French fare. Ordering food grilled, broiled, poached, or sautéed in wine such as a Bordelaise sauce is advisable. Watch out for those heavy cheese or cream sauces. Fish en papillote, a French favorite, is a delicious way to cook fish in its own juices.

Other Ethnic Choices

In Greek or Middle Eastern restaurants, hummus (garbanzo bean pâté with sesame butter, garlic, and lemon) and pita bread are usually available. Babaghanoush (eggplant pâté with sesame butter, garlic, and lemon) makes a great dip with vegetables. Tzatziki (yogurt and cucumber) is a good salad dressing. You can choose rice-based pilafs and tabbouleh (bulgur wheat, parsley, onion, tomato salad with olive oil and lemon). Salads that feature feta cheese (goat's cheese) are additional nutritious choices. Souvlaki (a combination of highly seasoned lamb and beef) is for those who like it hot, otherwise shish kabob with meat and vegetables is for tamer souls.

In Indian restaurants, tandoori chicken and lamb are good choices. Yogurt sauces and vegetables cooked in ghee (clarified butter) are permissable in small amounts. The pilafs, biryanis, dals (legume containing dishes) are delicious. Curry seasonings are healthful for those who can take a little heat. The pappadums (lentil wafers) are great munchies *if* they are baked, not fried. The same goes for chapatis and nan (garlic or onion bread).

Safe Flying

Call ahead at least twenty-four hours in advance to arrange for special food. Some airlines have diet menus approved by the American Heart Association. Others are also very accommodating for special dietary needs. You can usually order a cold seafood plate no matter which airline you fly, and be reasonably satisfied with what you get.

Cruising Cuisine

Like the airlines, the cruise lines also try to fulfill dietary requests made with a twenty-four-hour lead time. Leaner

luncheon and dinner entrees that meet the dietary guidelines of the American Heart Association are becoming
common fare among the more popular cruise lines.

Managing Margarine

The American Heart Association itself sponsors restaurants in every city of America that comply with their
low-fat, low-cholesterol, low-sodium dietary recommendations. Keep in mind, however, that low fat, low cholesterol does not mean good fat, because margarine is
still on the A.H.A. approved list. Request *no margarine*
on any of your foods, whatever you order. Low-fat, low-
cholesterol menus are a good start for most commercial
eateries. Just be careful and avoid the margarine!

Major cities such as Chicago, Baltimore, Palm Beach,
San Francisco, and Los Angeles are active participants
in the A.H.A. restaurant program. Many hotel chains
also participate. On the West Coast and the East Coast
you can usually find restaurants that serve A.H.A.
-approved meals. The menu will note A.H.A. approval.

APPENDIX

NUTRITION
EDUCATION
RESOURCES

Everyone should be his own physician.
We ought to assist, not force nature.
—Voltaire

We all need good self-care educational resources. Here are some of my favorites:

Biosocial Publications International
P.O. Box 1174
Tacoma, WA 98401
This organization provides two unusual nutrition-related journals. *The International Journal of Biosocial Research*, available semiannually, presents original studies and articles on how nutrition, biochemistry, and environment relate to human behavior. *The International Nutrition Review* is a quarterly publication that reports on current health research from around the world. The organization also has a catalog of carefully selected nutrition books that are relevant to many areas of nutritional science.

Candida Research and Information Foundation Newsletter
Candida Research and Information Foundation
P.O. Box 2719
Castro Valley, CA 94546
The newsletter is a well-substantiated source of information regarding immune suppression and chronic ill health. The organization explores the underlying causes of im-

mune dysfunction and offers information, reading lists, and nationwide physicians' referrals. Topics such as yeast/mold sensitivities, parasitic diseases, bowel flora, and allergy are covered in depth.

The Felix Letter
Clara Felix
P.O. Box 7094
Berkeley, CA 94707
The Felix Letter is a well researched, highly documented newsletter from nutritionist Clara Felix. Several issues deal with the importance of oils in the American diet. Ms. Felix provides a special slant, as a professional nutritionist, on many contemporary issues ranging from elixirs of youth to good versus bad prostaglandins. Her commentary on nutrition is laced with cartoons, photos, and original illustrations. Six to eight issues are published yearly.

The MegaHealth Society
P.O. Box 60637
Palo Alto, CA 94306
The MegaHealth Society is committed to the evaluation and explanation of state-of-the-art nutritional breakthroughs on issues of current concern. Such diverse topics as life extension, herpes virus, immunity, and brain enhancement are explored and discussed in language that is easy to understand. The Society also reports on trends and practices in the health food industry that affect consumers. The newsletter, *The Journal of the MegaHealth Society*, is published four times a year.

Nutrition Action Healthletter
Center for Science in the Public Interest
1501 16th Street NW
Washington, DC 20036
The *Nutrition Action Healthletter* is the monthly publication of C.S.P.I., a nonprofit organization that advocates health and environmental policies. The organization provides educational posters, books, pamphlets, public interest software, and kitchen gadgets. The C.S.P.I. staff is often quoted in nutritional magazines and newspapers on vari-

ous food-related issues. The C.S.P.I. is the public's "watch-dog" on the food industry.

Nutrition Health Review
171 Madison Avenue
New York, NY 10016
A newspaper-style review of nutrition, psychology, psychiatry, dentistry, and animal welfare gleaned from a wide variety of health professionals.

The Price Pottenger Nutrition Foundation
5871 El Cajon Bl.
San Diego, CA 92115
The foundation is based upon the work of two pioneering researchers, Weston A. Price, D.D.S., and Francis M. Pottenger, Jr., M.D. The organization researches, evaluates, and disseminates nutritional information in a quarterly journal. They are committed to promoting the link between high soil quality and high-level health. The classic Price text, *Nutrition and Physical Degeneration*, illustrates the degenerative illnesses that beset healthy primitive peoples when they adopt a typical modern diet. Similarly, the Pottenger Cat Studies demonstrate the importance of vital foods in preserving long-term health for humans and animals alike.

REFERENCES

Ames, B. "Dietary Carcinogens & Anti-Carcinogens": Oxygen Radicals and Degenerative Disease." *Science* 221 (1980): 1245.

Anderson, J., et al. "Oat bran intake selectively lowers serum low density lipoprotein cholesterol concentrations of hypercholesterolemic men." *American Journal of Clinical Nutrition* 34 (1981): 824.

————. "Hypocholesterolemic effects of oat bran or bean intake for hypercholesterolemic men." *American Journal of Clinical Nutrition* 40 (1984): 1146.

Beare-Rogers, J., et al. "The linoleic acid and trans fatty acids of margarines." *American Journal of Clinical Nutrition* 32 (1979): 1805.

Bieler, Henry, M.D. *Food Is Your Best Medicine.* (New York: Ballantine Books, 1984.)

"Biological Rhythms in Psychiatry and Medicine." National Institute of Mental Health. National Clearinghouse for Mental Health Information, pp. 120–32.

BioSyn Position Paper. "The GLA and ALA Connection." BioSyn, Marblehead, MA 01945.

Bland, Jeffrey, Ph.D. *Your Health Under Siege.* (Brattleboro, VT: The Stephen Green Press, 1981.)

Bordia, A., et al. "Effect of the essential oils of garlic and onion on alimentary hyperlipidemia." *Atherosclerosis* 21 (1975): 15.

Brodeur, Paul. *The Zapping of America.* (New York: Norton, 1977.)

Brown, M. "Fast Foods Are Hazardous to Your Health." *Science Digest*, April 1986: 31.

Burkitt, D. "Some Neglected Leads to Cancer Causation." *Journal of the National Cancer Institute*, 47, no. 4 (1971): 913.

Clement, Mark. *Aluminum: A Menace to Health.* (Sussex, England: Health Science Press, 1971.)

Crawford, M.A., et al. "Essential fatty acid requirements in infancy." *AJCN* 31 (1978): 2181–85.

Cheraskin, Emanuel, M.D., D.M.D., and W. Ringsdorf, Jr., D.M.D., M.S., with Arline Brecher. *Psychodietetics.* (New York: Stein and Day, 1974.)

Crapper, Dr., et al. "Essential fatty acid requirements in infancy." *AJCN* 31 (1978): 2181–85.

Crook, William, M.D. *The Yeast Connection.* (Jackson, Tennessee: Professional Books, 1984.)

Dyerberg, J., and H. O. Bang. "Eicosapentaenoic acid and prevention of thrombosis and atherosclerosis?" *Lancet* 2 (1978): 117.

————. "Lipid metabolism, atherogenesis and haemostasis in Eskimos; the role of the prostaglandin-3 family." *Haemostasis* 8 (1979): 227.

En-Trophy Institute Review 4 (March 6, 1980). "The Dietary Maginot Line." Community Nutrition Institute.

Erickson, D. R., ed., et al. *Handbook of Soy Oil Processing and Utilization.* Third printing. (St. Louis, Missouri and Champaign, Illinois: American Soybean Association and American Oil Chemists' Society, 1985.)

Erlander, Stig, Ph.D. *Dr. Erlander's Pathway to Health.* (Altadena, CA: P.O. Box 106, Altadena, CA, 1980.)

"Facts About Food Poisoning" FDA Consumer Memo. Washington, DC: DHEW Publication No. (FDA) 74–2046 (April 1974).

Freidman, Meyer. *Treating Type A Behavior and Your Heart.* (New York; Alfred A. Knopf, 1984.)

Gibson, R. A., and G. M. Kneebone. "Fatty acid composition of human colostrum and human breast milk." *American Journal of Clinical Nutrition* 34 (1981): 252–57.

Grundy, S. "Comparison of Monosaturated Fatty Acids and Carbohydrates for Lowering Plasma Cholesterol." *New England Journal of Medicine* 314, no. 12 (1986): 745.

Haflick, L. "On Those Magical Prostaglandins." *Executive Health* 16 (1980): 8.

Hall, Ross Hume. *Food For Nought.* (New York: Harper & Row, 1974.)

Health From the Sun Position Papers. "EPA Containing Marine Oils—a Consumer's Guide," "Evening Primrose Oil—a Guide for the Consumer," and "Technical Specifications of Edible Oils—a Consumer's Guide." Health from the Sun Products, Inc. Needham Heights, MA 02194.

Health Research. *The Story of Aluminum Poisoning.* Health Research, Mokelumne Hill, CA 95245.

Hepburn, F. N., et al. "Provisional tables on the content of omega-3 fatty acids and other fat components of selected foods." *Journal of the American Dietetic Association* 86 (1986): 788–93.

Himms, Hagen, J. "Thermogenesis in Brown Adipose Tissue as an Energy Buffer." *New England Journal of Medicine* 311 (1984): 1549.

Hirai, A., et al. "Eicosapentaenoic acid and platelet function in Japanese." *Lancet* 2 (1985): 1132.

Holman, R. T., ed. *Progress in Lipid Research.* Vol. 20. (New York: Pergamon Press, 1982.)

———, et al. "Effects of trans fatty acid isomers upon essential fatty acid deficiency in rats." *Proceedings of the Society for Experimental Biology and Medicine* 93 (1956): 175–79.

———, et al. *Dietary Fats and Health.* E.G. Perkins and W. J. Visek, eds. (Champaign, IL: American Oil Chemists Society Press, 1983.)

Horrobin, David F., M.D., Ph.D. *Clinical Uses of Essential Fatty Acids.* (Montreal-London: Eden Press, 1982.)

———, et al. "The nutritional regulation of T-lymphocyte function." *Medical Hypothesis* 5 (1979): 969.

———. "Schizophrenia: the role of abnormal essential fatty acid and prostaglandin metabolism." Rev. *Drug Metabolism Drug Interaction* 4 (1983): 339.

———. "The regulation of prostaglandin biosynthesis by the manipulation of essential fatty acid metabolism." Rev. *Drug Metabolism Drug Interaction* 4 (1983): 339.

Howell, Edward. *Enzyme Nutrition.* (Wayne, NJ: Avery, 1985.)

Hunter, Beatrice Trum. *How Safe Is Food in Your Kitchen?* (New York: Scribner's, 1981.)

———. "Gluten Intolerance." Presentation of American Academy of Environmental Medicine, October 1986.

Jones, Jeanne. *Food Lovers Diet.* (San Francisco: 101 Productions, 1982.)

Kinderlehrer, J. "B6—Maybe the answer to heart disease." *Prevention,* September 1979: 138.

Kinsella, J. E., et al. "Metabolism of trans fatty acids with emphasis on the prostaglandins." *American Journal of Clinical Nutrition* 34 (1981): 2307.

Kremer, J. M., et al. "Effects of manipulation of dietary fatty acids on clinical manifestations of rheumatoid arthritis." *Lancet* 184 (1985).

Kummerow, F. A., et al. "Saturated Fat and Cholesterol: Dietary 'Risk-Factors' or Essentials to Human Life?" *Food and Nutrition News*, September-October 1981.

———. "Nutrition imbalance and angiotoxins as dietary risk factors in coronary heart disease." *American Journal of Clinical Nutrition* 32 (1979): 58–83.

Lau, B., et al. "Allium (Garlic) and Atherosclerosis: A Review." *Nutrition Research* 3 (1983): 119.

Lecos, C. "Safety Tips for the Outdoor Chef." *Health Connections Magazine*, July 1985: 8.

Lee, Tak. H., et al. "Effect of dietary enrichment with Icosapentaenoic and Dicosahexaenoic acids on in vitro neutrophil and monocyte leukotriene generation and neutrophil function." *New England Journal of Medicine* 312 (1985): 1217.

Kugler, Hans, M.D. *Dr. Kugler's Seven Keys to a Longer Life.* (New York: Stein and Day, 1978.)

Lovell, C. R., et al. "Treatment of Atopic Eczema with Evening Primrose Oil." *Lancet* 278 (1981).

Lyinsky, W., et al. "Benzo-pyrene and Other Polynuclear Hydrocarbons in Charbroiled Meat." *Science* 145 (1985): 2.

Mann, John A. *Secrets of Life Extension.* (Berkeley: And/or Press, 1980.)

May, John. *Curious Facts.* (New York: Holt, Rinehart and Winston, 1980.)

McCully, K., et al. "Production of Arteriosclerosis by Homocysteinemia." *American Journal of Pathology* 61, no. 1 (1970): 1.

"Obesity Linked to Metabolism in Brown Fat." *Chemical Engineering News*, February 16, 1981: 25.

Ornish, Dean, M.D. *Stress, Diet, and Your Heart.* (New York: Holt, Rinehart and Winston, 1983.)

Oski, Frank, M.D. *Don't Drink Your Milk.* (Syracuse, NY: Mollica Press, Ltd., 1983.)

Oster, K. "Predisposition to atherosclerosis" letter. *Journal of the American Medical Association* 222 (1972): 704.

Oster, Kurt A., M.D., and Donald J. Ross, Ph.D. *Homogenized Milk May Cause Your Heart Attack: The XO Factor.* (New York: Park City Press, 1983.)

Ott, John N. *Health and Light.* (New York: Pocket Books, 1976.)

Page, Melvin, D.D.S. *Chemistry in Health and Disease.* (La Mesa, CA: Price Pottenger Foundation Reprint, 1984.)

Passwater, Richard, Ph.D. *Evening Primrose Oil.* New Canaan, CT: Keats Publishing, 1981.)

Pearce, M., et al. "Incidence of cancer in men on a diet high in polyunsaturated fat." *Lancet* 464 (1971).

Pennington, Jean A. T., and Helen Nichols Church. *Bowes and Church's Food Values of Portions Commonly Used.* (Philadelphia: J. B. Lippincott Company, 1985.)

Phillipson, B., and William E. Connor, et al. "Reduction of plasma lipids, lipoproteins, and apoproteins by dietary fish oils in patients with hypertriglyceridemia." *New England Journal of Medicine* 312 (1985): 1210.

Pinckney, Edward, M.D., and D. Pinckney. *The Cholesterol Controversy.* (Los Angeles: Sherbourne Press, Inc., 1973.)

———. "The potential toxicity of excessive polyunsaturates." *American Heart Journal* 85 (1973): 723.

Pritikin, Nathan, with J. Patrick McCrady. *The Pritikin Program for Diet and Exercise.* (New York: Grosset and Dunlap, 1979.)

Raloff, J. "Oxidized Lipids: a Key to Heart Disease." *Science News* 129:278.

———. "Reason for Boning Up on Manganese." *Science News*, September 27, 1986.

Randolph, Theron, G., M.D., and Ralph W. Moss, Ph.D. *An Alternative Approach to Allergies.* (New York: Bantam, 1981.)

Rendelman, R. "Dr. Edward Howell: a Man with an Urgent Message." *Bestways Magazine*, May 1979, reprint.

Rinkel, H. J. "Food Allergy: The Role of Food Allergy in Internal Medicine." *Annals Allergy* 2 (1944):115–124.

Rowe, A. H. *Food Allergy, Its Manifestations, Diagnosis and Treatment.* (Philadelphia:1983.)

Rudin, D. "The Major Psychoses and Neurosis as Omega-3 Essential Fatty Acid Deficiency Syndrome: Substrate Beriberi." *Med. Hypotheses* 8 (1982): 17.

Schroeder, Henry A. *The Poisons Around Us.* (Bloomington, IN: Indiana University Press, 1974.)

Shurkin, Joel. "Artificial sweeteners." *Healthline*, October 1983:10.

Taub, Harald J. *Keeping Healthy in a Polluted World.* (New York: Harper & Row, 1974.)

Taylor, C. B., et al. "Spontaneously Occurring Angiotoxic Derivatives of Cholesterol." *American Journal of Clinical Nutrition* 32 (1979): 40.

Thomas, L. "Mortality from arteriosclerotic disease and consumption of hydrogenated oils and fats." *Brit. J. Preven. Soc. Med.* 29 (1975): 82.

Thomas, L. H. "Hydrogenated oils and fats: the presence of chemically modified fatty acids in human adipose tissue." *A.J.C.N.* 34 (1981): 877–86.

Toufexis, A. "Dieting: the Losing Game." *Time*, January 20, 1986:54.

Truss, C. Orian. *The Missing Diagnosis.* (Birmingham, AL: P.O. Box 26508, Birmingham, 35226. 1983.)

―――. "The Role of Candida Albicans in Human Illness." *Journal of Orthomolecular Psychiatry* 10, no. 4 (1981).

U.S. Department of Agriculture. *Composition of Foods, Fats and Oils, Raw, Processed, Prepared.* USDA Agricultural Handbook No. 8-4, 1979.

U.S. Department of Health, Education and Welfare. *Healthy People: The Surgeon General's Report on Health Promotion and Disease Prevention.* (Washington, DC: Government Printing Office, 1979.)

U.S. Senate Select Committee on Nutrition and Human Needs. *Dietary Goals for the United States.* Second edition. (Washington, DC: Government Printing Office, 1977.)

Vaddadi, K. S., and D. F. Horrobin. "Weight loss produced by evening primrose oil administration in normal and schizophrenic individuals." *IRCS Medical Science* (1979):52.

Wurtman, Richard J. "The effects of light on the human body." *Scientific American* 233, no. 1 (July 1975): 68–77.

INDEX

A

Aerobic exercise, 89–92, 94, 153
Aerobics Center, The, 92
Agar-agar, 127
Airplane meals, 219
ALA (alpha-linolenic acid), 42
Alcohol, 71, 95, 142–143
  organic, sources of, 134
  recommended types and
    brands, 127
Allicin, 80, 82
Almond oil, 93
  recommended brands, 120
Alpha-linolenic acid. *See* ALA
Aluminum, 112–113
Alzheimer's disease, 112
Amaranth, 201
Amazing Facts, 57
American Heart Association, xvi,
  15, 66, 219, 220
American Journal of Nutrition,
  64
*American Physician Family
  Journal, The*, 144
Anderson, James, 85
Anderson Hospital and Tumor
  Institute, 80
Anemia, 66
Angostura bitters, 209
Antacids, 112
Antioxidants, 29, 30
Apples, 104
Archer, Douglas, 98
Arthritis, 7, 9, 45
Ascriptin, aluminum in, 112
Aspartame, 127

Aspergillus niger, 80
Asthma, 9
Avidin, 107
Avocado oil, 55

B

Back to Basic entrees, 128
Baking, 108
Baking powder, recommended
  brands, 125
Baking soda
  sodium in, 116
  vitamin destruction, 97
Bang, H.O., 3
Bantus, 2
Beans, 84, 106–107
  organic, suppliers of, 130, 132,
    134, 135
  recommended types, 125–126
  seasoning for, 213
  storage, 126
Beef, 123
  organic suppliers of, 130, 133,
    134, 135, 136, 137
  see also Recipe Index
Beef tallow, 58, 95
Bellevue Hospital, xx
Beta carotene, 30, 79, 94
Beverages, 127
  see also specific beverage
Bicycling, 92
Bieler, Henry, 68–70
Bile, 59, 84
Biosocial Publications Interna-
  tional, 221
BioSyn, 78

Blackberries, 104
Black currant oil, 74
Blueberries, 104
Borage, 5, 74
Bordia, Arun, 81
Bowel disorders, 84, 113
Brain disorders, 46
Brains (food), 74
Bran, oat, 84, 85, 209
Breads
    organic, suppliers of, 132, 135
    recommended brands and
        storage, 125
Breast-feeding, 76
Brine, 116
Broiling, 108
Bufferin, aluminum in, 112
Burger King, 59
Burkitt, Denis, 85, 86
Business Trend Analysts, Inc., 59
Butter, 64, 146

C
Cajun spices, supplier of, 214
Calcium, 13, 27, 31, 112
Calories, fat percentage list,
    38–39
Cancer
    colon, 84
    cooking methods related to,
        109–110
    diet and, 10
    essential fat inhibition of, 7
    fish oils in prevention of,
        44
    garlic oil to inhibit, 80
    indoles against, 80
Candida albicans, xxii, 7, 14, 80,
    116–117
Candida Research and Informa-
    tion Foundation, 221–222
Canning, 97, 100
Canola oil, 56–57
Carbohydrates
    complex, 11
    exchange list, 205–208
    refined, 71

Cardiovascular disease
    aerobic exercise to prevent,
        89–90
    fish oil and, 9, 44
    heat-damaged oils and, 64
    rate of, xvi
    and serum cholesterol, 2, 7,
        66–67
Carpaccio, 105
Caveman's Diet, 13
Celiac disease. See Gluten,
    intolerance
Cell membranes, 26
Center for Science in the Public
    Interest, 117, 222–223
Cereals
    organic, suppliers of, 132, 134,
        135
    recommended brands, 124
Charcoal grilling, 109–110
Cheese, 95, 135, 136, 137
Chewing food, 118–119
Chicken. See Poultry; Recipe
    Index
Chinese food, 218
Cholesterol
    and cardiovascular disease, 2,
        7, 66–70
    function, 63
    level in blood, 65–67, 68–69,
        85
    lipoproteins and, 65
    oxidation of, 64, 95
    serum, 2, 7, 18
    sources, 47, 64
    stress and, 66
Chopping boards, 97, 112
Cigarettes. See Tobacco
Cis fatty acids, 28, 29
Clorox, 102, 112
    cleansing formula, 128–129
Coconut oil, 57, 58, 74, 95
Coffee, 71, 141–142
    decaffeinated, 142
    substitutes, 127
Colon cancer, 84
Columbia University, xx

Community Nutrition Institute, 52
Condiments, 126
Connecticut College, xx
Connor, William, 6
Convenience foods, 59–60
  see also Fast foods
Cooking, 97, 99, 100
  fish, fowl, and meat, 105
  fruit, 104
  recommended methods and utensils, 107–109, 110–113
  seeds, peanuts, nuts, beans, egg whites and potatoes, 106–107
  undesirable methods and utensils, 109–110, 111–113
  vegetables, 103–104
Cookware. See Utensils, cooking; types
Copper cookware, 112
Corning Ware, 111
Corn oil, 74, 93
  recommended brands, 120–121
Cottonseed oil, 58, 74, 116
Crackers, recommended brands, 124
Cranberry juice, 19, 152
Cranberry sauce, 209
Crisco, 51
Crook, William, 13
Cutting boards, 97, 112

D
Dairy products
  exchange list, 208
  on New Nutrition Diet, 140–141
  recommended brands, 122
  storage, 122
  see also specific product
Dairy tin bakeware, 113
Dancing, 91
Death, causes of, 34–35
Deepbrook Associates, xx
Deodorants, 113

Department of Health and Human Sciences, 34
Desgrey, J. Maxwell, xxii
Detoxification, xxii, 152–154
DHA (docosahexaenoic acid), 3
Diabetes, 7, 10, 44, 66, 86
Diarrhea, 12
Dietary Goals for the United States, 10
Dietary supplements, 76–78, 94, 143–145, 151
Diets
  fad, 34
  high carbohydrate, 12
  see also New Nutrition Diet; Pritikin Nutrition Program
Di-Gel, aluminum in, 112
Digestion, 119–120
Docosahexaenoic acid. See DHA
Drugs and drug products. See medications; specific kinds
Dry eye, 46
Dryerberg, John, 3

E
Educational resources, 221–223
EFA support, 78
Eggs
  avidin in, 107
  cholesterol and cooking method, 64–65
  Clorox bath for, 129
  dried, 95
  enzyme inhibitors in, 107
  organic, suppliers of, 135, 136
  seasoning for, 213
  see also Recipe Index
Eicosapentaenoic acid. See EPA
Enamel cookware, 111
Enzymatic cofactors, 42
EPA (eicosapentaenoic acid), 3, 6, 41–42, 75–78, 94
Equivalents, food, 202–208
Eskimos, xvi, xvii, 3, 44

Essential fats
   benefits of, 6–7
   defined, 49–50
   in Fat Flush program, 19
   necessity for, 5
   in New Nutrition Diet, xvii,
      5–6, 18
   prostaglandins, transformation
      into, 42
   sources of, xvii, 5, 76–78
   see also Omega-3 fatty acids;
      Omega-6 fatty acids
Ethnic dining, 217–219
Evening primrose oil, 5, 35, 74
Exchange lists, 202–208
Exercise plan, 20, 89–92, 94
Extracts, flavor, 126
Eye. See Retina; Tear production

F
Fad diets, 34
Fast foods, 58–59, 64
Fasting, xxii
Fat, body
   brown, 17–18, 35–37
   white, 17, 36
Fat, dietary
   basic groups, 24–25
   calories, percentage of, 38–39
   in convenience foods, 61
   damaged, 15–16, 23, 28–30,
      69–71, 95
   exchange list, 202–203
   food label terminology,
      115–116
   functions of, 26–27
   monounsaturated, 25, 55–56
   in Pritikin diet, 2, 3, 6, 8
   saturated, 24–25, 57–59, 67, 95
   see also Essential fats; GLA;
      Omega-3 fatty acids;
      Omega-6 fatty acids; Polyun-
      saturated fats
Fat Flush program, 19, 149–156
FDA (Food and Drug Administration), 98
Felix Letter, The, 222

Fermented foods, 13
Fiber, 19, 59, 83–87, 94
Fingernails, 7, 11
Fish
   canned, 122
   Clorox bath for, 129
   cooking and storing, 105
   raw, 105
   recommended types, 94, 122,
      123
   seasoning for, 212
   shellfish, 106, 123
   see also Oils, fish; Recipe
      Index
Fish Oil. See Oils, fish
Flavor extracts, 126
Flaxseed, 209
Flours, 125
   organic, suppliers of, 132, 134,
      135
Foil, aluminum, 112, 113
Folic acid, 12
Food Is Your Best Medicine,
   68
Food poisoning, 97–98
Food preparation and storage,
   96–113
Food Values of Portions
   Commonly Used, 144
Fowl. See Poultry
Free radicals, 30, 79
Freezing, 97, 100
French food, 218
Friedman, Meyer, 66
Frozen dinners, 60–61
Fruit
   citrus, 79
   Clorox bath for, 129
   exchange list, 204–205
   exotic, 194
   on Fat Flush program, 151
   fiber source, 85
   juice, 72
   on New Nutrition Diet,
      139–140
   organic, suppliers of, 130, 136
   preparation and cooking, 104

Fruit (*continued*)
  preserves, 124
  recommended, 94, 123–124
  seasoning for, 213–214
  selection and storage, 101–102,
    103
  sugar source, 72
  see also specific fruit; Recipe
    Index
Frying, 109
Full-spectrum light, xxii, 20, 91,
  92

G
Gamma linolenic acid. *See*
  GLA
Garlic, 80–82
  organic, suppliers of, 130, 131,
    132
Gas stoves, 110
Gelatin, 127
Gelusil, aluminum in, 112
Giardia lamblia, 113
GLA (gamma linolenic acid)
  cis-linolenic acid conversion,
    36–37
  prostaglandin component,
    41–43
  sources, 3, 6, 42, 74
  supplements, 78, 94
  treatment with, 14–15
Glass cookware, 111
Gluten
  grains containing, 11
  grains without, 13
  intolerance, 11–12, 86
Goat's milk, 208
Gooseberry oil, 74
Grains
  basic recipe, 201
  exotic, 201
  fiber content, 84
  gluten-free, 13
  organic, suppliers of, 132, 134,
    135, 136
  soaking, 107
  sprouts, 76

  recommended types and
    brands, 124
  storage, 124
  whole, 11–12, 79, 94
Greek food, 219
Grilling, 109–110
Grundy, Scott M., 56
Gurewich, Victor, 81

H
Harvard Medical School, 9
Hazelnut oil, 93
  recommended brands,
    120–121
HDL (high-density lipoproteins),
  65
Health and Energy Institute, The,
  137
Health food stores, 117–118
Heart disease. *See* Cardiovascu-
  lar disease
Heat processing, 28, 37
Herbs, 126, 211–214
  organic, suppliers of, 132, 133,
    135
Hill Health Center, xx
Hoffman-LaRoche, 4
Homogenization, 30–32, 37, 95
Horrobin, David, 3, 6
Horseradish, 209
Hydrogenation, 28–29, 37, 50–52,
  95
Hydroponics, 101–102
Hypercholestremia, 68
Hypertension, 11

I
Immune system, 7
Indian food, 219
Indoles, 80
*International Journal of Biosocial
  Research, The*, 221
*International Nutrition Review,
  The*, 221
Iron, 13, 111
Irradiated food, 137
Italian food, 217

J
Jogging. *See* Running
*Journal of the American Medical
　Association*, 66, 89
Juice, fruit, 72
　see also Cranberry juice

K
Kentucky Medical Center, 85
Kidneys (food), 74
Kummerow, Fred, 52

L
Labels, food, 115–117
Lamb, 123
Lancet, 3
Lard, 58
L-carnitine, 79
LDL (low-density lipoproteins),
　65
Lecithin, 29, 79
Legumes. *See* Beans; Lentils;
　Peas
Lentils, 84
Light, full-spectrum, xxii, 20, 91,
　92
Linseed oil, 120
Lipid Research Clinic's Coronary
　Primary Prevention Trial,
　66
Lipids, 24
Lipoproteins, 65
Live Longer Now, xix,
　10
Liver (food), 74
Liver disease, 66, 72
Long Life Cocktail, 19, 151
Lucite, 112
Lysine, 201

M
Maalox, aluminum in, 112
Mademoiselle (magazine), 60
Magnesium, 42, 94
Manganese, 31–32
Margarine, 50–53, 95, 220
Master Formula, 19, 157–158

Master Menu Plan, 19, 146,
　159–169
Mayonnaise, 122
Mazola oil, 64
McCully, Kilmer, 80
McDonald's, 57, 59
McManus, Bruce, 67
Meat
　Clorox bath for, 129
　food poisoning from, 97–98
　lean red, 74
　organic sources of, 135, 136,
　　137
　preparation and storage,
　　105–106
　raw, 105
　seasoning for, 212–213
　see also specific meat
Meat and poultry hotline, 106
Medications, 112, 144
　see also specific brand
　　names
MegaHealth Society, The, 222
Menstruation. *See* PMS
Menus, 159–169
　see also Recipe Index
Metabolism, 34, 69, 90
Metamucil, 151
Mexican food, 218
Microwave, 108–109
Milk, 30–32, 64, 76, 95, 99, 208,
　209
Mineral oil, 116
Minerals. *See* Dietary supple-
　ments; specific mineral
Monounsaturated fats, 25, 55–56
MSG (monosodium glutamate),
　116
Multiple sclerosis, 45
Myelin, 26
Mylanta, aluminum in, 112

N
National Academy of Sciences,
　10
National Heart, Lung and Blood
　Institute, 67

National Institutes of Health, 65

New England Journal of Medicine, xv, 6, 9, 56

New Nutrition Diet
  Fat Flush program, 150–156
  fats, xvi, xvii, 5–6, 73–78
  Master Formula, 19, 157–158
  Master Menu Plan, 19, 146, 159–169
  nutritional discoveries, 96
  questions about, 139–147
  recipes. *See* Recipe Index
  recommended foods and brands, 120–128
  restaurant and travel trips, 215–220
  Ten-Point Prescription, 147–148
  transitional tips, 208–209
  weight loss on, 16–17, 145–146

Newsletters, 221–223

New York Friars Club, xxii

New York Institute of Dietetics, xx

Niacin. *See* Vitamins, B-3

Nursing. *See* Breast-feeding

Nutrition Action Healthletter, 60, 222–223

Nutrition and Physical Degeneration, 223

Nutrition Health Review, 223

NutriWheat, 86, 87

Nuts, 74, 107
  organic, sources of, 134, 135, 136
  recommended types, 121–122
  storage, 122

O

Oat bran, 84, 85, 209

Obesity, 33, 34–35, 67
  see also Weight loss

Oils, fish
  capsules, 77–78
  and cardiovascular disease, 9, 44
  EPA content of, 75
  in Eskimo diet, xvii, 3
  see also Omega headings

Oils, vegetable
  chemical extraction, 48, 49
  cold pressed, 48–49, 55
  crude, 49
  early production methods, 48
  expeller pressed, 49, 93
  in fast foods, 58–59
  on Fat Flush program, 150, 155
  heat-damaged, 64
  monounsaturated, 55–56
  polyunsaturated, 47–53, 58
  processed, 37, 47, 49
  recommended, 93, 120–121
  saturated, 57
  storage, 121
  unprocessed, xvii, 74, 93
  see also specific oil

Oleo. *See* Margarine

Oliphant, Ann, xxii

Oliphant, Harry, xxii

Olive oil, 6, 55–56, 74, 93
  recommended brands, 121

Omega-3 fatty acids
  DHA (docosahexaenoic acid), 3
  disease treatment with, 14–15
  EPA (eicosapentaenoic acid), 3, 6, 41–42, 75–76
  in primitive diets, xv–xvi
  prostaglandin formation, 4
  sources, xvii, 5, 25, 75–76

Omega-6 fatty acids
  in American diet, xvi
  disease treatment with, 14–15
  prostaglandin formation, 4
  sources, 5, 25
  see also GLA

Onions, 81–82
  organic, supplier of, 136

Oregon Health Sciences University, 9

Organic food suppliers, 130–137

Organic Merchants Association, 47

Ornish, Dean, 66

Osteoporosis, 31, 112

Oster, Kurt A., 30–31

Oxidation, 29–30, 37, 64, 95

P

Pabirin, aluminum in, 112

Pain relievers, 112

Palm kernel oil, 57, 58, 95

Palm oil, 57, 58, 95

Parasites, 105

Parchment paper, cooking in, 113

Pasta
exchange list, 208
organic, suppliers of, 130, 132, 135, 136
recommended brands, 125

PCBs (polychlorinated biphenyls), 77, 78

Peanut oil, 6, 55, 56, 74, 93
recommended brands, 120–121

Peanuts, 106–107

Peas, dried, 84

PMS (premenstrual syndrome), 7

Pollution, environmental, 144

Polysystemic chronic candidiasis, 13

Polyunsaturated fats
dangers of, 15, 70–71
processing of, 47–53
sources, 25

Potatoes, 102, 106–107, 133

Poultry, 98, 105–106, 123
Clorox bath for, 129
cooking and storage, 105–106
organic, suppliers of, 130, 135, 136
recommended types and brands, 123
salmonella infection of, 98
seasoning for, 213

Premenstrual syndrome. See PMS

Preserves, fruit, 124

Pressure cooking, 110

Price Pottenger Nutrition Foundation, 223

Pritikin, Nathan
cardiac-risk reduction, xv, xix
death of, 9
fat content of diet, 2, 3, 5, 6, 8, 21
kindness of, xxi
personal health, xvi, 1–2
research, 2

Pritikin Longevity Centers, xvi, xvii, xix-xxii, 9

Pritikin Nutrition Program
basics of, 1–2
disadvantages, xvii, 11–14
successes, 10

Pritikin Program for Diet and Exercise, The, 3

Procter & Gamble, 51

Prostaglandins
benefits of, 44–46
function of, xvii, 4, 41
inflammatory, 45, 56, 70
production of, 26, 42–43

Protein
exchange list, 203
on Fat Flush program, 150
recommended sources, 122–123

Publications, nutrition, 221–223

Puritan oil, 64

Pyrex cookware, 111, 113

Q

Quinoa, 201

R

Recipes. See Recipe Index

Refrigeration, 99–101

Restaurant dining, 215–220

Retina, 20

Riboflavin. See Vitamins, B-2

Rice bran oil, 74

Rolaids, aluminum in, 112
Rudin, Donald, 6
Running, 90–91

S
SAD (seasonal affective disorder), 91
Safflower oil, 36, 74, 93
  recommended brands, 120–121
Salt, 116
  recommended types and brands, 126
Saltman, Paul, 31
Saturated fats, 24–25, 58–59, 67, 95
Sautéing, 107
Sears, Barry, 6
Seasonings. See Herbs; Spices
Seeds
  ALA source, 76
  enzyme inhibitors in, 107
  organic, suppliers of, 132, 134, 135
  recommended types, 121–122
  storage, 122
Selenium, 30, 79, 94
Senate Select Committee on Nutrition and Human Needs, 10
Sesame oil, 74, 93
  recommended brands, 120–121
Shellfish, 106, 123
Shipboard meals, 219–220
Shopping, 117–118
Shortening, 51, 95
Skin diseases, 7, 45
Smoking. See Tobacco
Sodium, 116, 140
Soft drinks, 143
Solanine, 102
Soups, 126
  seasoning for, 213
  see also Recipe Index
Soy oil, 74
  recommended brands, 120–121
Soy sauce, 116, 209
Spicer, Arnold, 86

Spicer's International, 87, 128
Spices, 126, 132, 211–214
  Cajun, supplier of, 214
Spittle, Constance, 79
Sprouts, grain, 76
Sprue disease. See Gluten, intolerance
Stainless steel cookware, 110–111, 113
Steak tartare, 105
Steaming, 107–108
  timetable for vegetables, 190–192
Stir-fry, 107
Stoves, gas, 110
Stress, 66, 67
Stress, Diet and Your Heart, 66
Sugar, 71, 95, 117
Sunflower oil, 74, 93
  recommended brands, 120–121
Sunglasses, 20
Sunlight, 20
Surgeon General's Report on Health Promotion and Disease Prevention, 10
Sushi, 105
Swanson, Gloria, 68
Sweetbreads, 74
Sweeteners, 126–127
Swimming, 92

T
Tamari, 116
Tarahumara Indians, 2, 11
Taylor, C.B., 64
Tear production, 46
Ten-Point Prescription, 147–148
Thiamin. See Vitamins, B-1
Thickeners, 125
Thyroid gland, 66
Toasting, 108
Tobacco, 67, 144
Tofu, 123
Trans fatty acids
  cis form converted to, 28, 29

Trans fatty acids (*continued*)
  prostaglandin blockers, 52,
    71
  sources, 37, 59, 95
Triglycerides, 7, 71–72
Truss, Orian, 13
Tufts University, 81
Twain, Mark, 118

U
University of Leiden, 9
University of Nebraska Medical
    Center, 67
University of Texas Health
    Sciences Center, 56
U.S. Department of Agriculture,
    106
Utensils, cooking, 110–113

V
Vanquish, aluminum in,
    112
Veal, 123
Vegetable oil. *See* Oils,
  vegetable
Vegetables
  Clorox bath for, 129
  cruciferous, 79
  deep yellow, 79
  exchange list, 203–204
  exotic, 189
  on Fat Flush program,
    150
  fiber content, 85
  green leafy, 74, 76, 79
  organic, suppliers of, 130–137
  preparation and cooking,
    103–104
  recommended, 94, 123
  seasoning for, 213
  selecting and storing,
    101–103
  steaming timetable, 190–192
  see also Oils, vegetable;
    specific vegetable; Recipe
    Index
Vinegars, 126, 136

Vitamins
  A, 8, 13, 27, 45
  B group, 12, 27, 99, 107
  B-1 (thiamin), 104, 106
  B-2 (riboflavin), 99
  B-3 (niacin), 42, 79, 94
  B-6, 37, 42, 80, 94
  B-12, 12
  C, 30, 42, 79, 94
  D, 27
  E, 8, 13, 27, 30, 79, 94
  fat fighters, 78–79
  fat soluble, 8, 13, 27
  food storage and preparation,
    97, 98–99
  K, 27
  organic, supplier of, 135
  see also Dietary
    supplements

W
Walking, 90–91
Walnut Acres, 61, 87
  address, 136
  recommended products, 120,
    122, 124, 126
Walnut oil, 74, 93
  recommended brands,
    120–121
Wargovich, Michael J., 80
Water
  chlorinated, 144
  contaminated, 113
  on Fat Flush program, 151,
    153–154
  filtered, 127
  on New Nutrition Diet,
    94
Water filter, 127, 128
Weight loss, 6, 16–17, 35,
    145–146
Wheat. *See* Grains
Whiote, Michael, 67
Women, Infants, and Children
    Food Program, xx
Wood chopping board, 112
Worcestershire sauce, 209

X
Xanthine oxidase. *See* XO
XO, 30–31, 32

Y
Yeast
  Aspergillus niger, 80
  Candida albicans, xxii,
    7, 14, 80, 116–117

foods related to, 13,
  117
systemic infection, 45,
  116–117
Yogurt, 95, 209

Z
Zinc, 42, 45, 79, 94
Zyliss food slicer, 111

RECIPE INDEX

A
Apple, baked, 195
Applesauce, 196
Artichoke omelet, 187–188

B
Beef
  brisket of beef dinner,
    183–184
  Mediterranean meatballs, 181
  stuffed peppers oreganato,
    182
Black bean soup, 176
Blueberry banana sorbet, 200
Bombay curry sauce, 171–172
Brisket of beef dinner, 183–184

C
Cajun cod, 180
Carob gelatin, 199–200
Carrots and snow peas, minted,
  193
Cherry gelatin, 199
Chicken
  with sherry dijon, 180
  and vegetable sauté, five spice,
    185
Chickpea sesame pâté, 174
Chili mayonnaise, 172
Coconut rum pudding, 197–198
Coleslaw, 194
Cranberry juice, 152

D
Desserts. See Fruit; Gelatins;
  Puddings; Sorbets

Dressings, Salad. See Salad
  dressings and sauces

E
Eggs
  artichoke omelet, 187–188
  spinach fritatta, 188
Equivalents, food, 202–208
Eskimo salad niçoise, 184

F
Fish
  Cajun cod, 180
  halibut, lemon-baked, 182–183
  halibut shrimp kabob, 187
  salmon, baked in wine,
    185–186
  salmon croquettes, 181–182
  salmon loaf, spiced, 186
  tuna, grilled, 186–187
French olive oil dressing,
  170
Fruit
  apple, baked, 195
  applesauce, 196
  pears, vanilla, 195
  rhubarb sauce, 196
  see also Gelatins; Sorbets
Fruit compote pudding, 198

G
Garlic roasted peppers and
  anchovies, 193
Gazpacho, 177–178
Gelatins
  carob, 199–200

Gelatins (*continued*)
  cherry, 199
  piña colada, 199
  pomegranate, 199
Ginger pear sorbet, 200–201
Grain recipe, basic, 201
Greek lentil soup, 177

H
Halibut, lemon-baked, 182–183
Halibut shrimp kabob, 187
Hazelnut dressing, 169
Hollandaise, 172–173
Horseradish sauce with dill, 173

J
Jack's party pâté, 174–175

L
Long Life Cocktail, 151

M
Maple pudding, 198
Mediterranean meatballs, 181
Muffin, magic, 196–197

P
Pâtés
  chickpea sesame pâté, 174
  Jack's party pâté, 174–175
  sweetheart pâté, 175–176
Peanut dressing with ginger and garlic, 170–171
Pears, vanilla, 195
Peppers and anchovies, garlic roasted, 193
Peppers oreganato, stuffed, 182
Piña colada gelatin, 199
Pomegranate gelatin, 199
Poultry. *See* Chicken
Puddings
  coconut rum, 197–198
  fruit compote, 198
  maple, 198
  tapioca, 198–199

R
Ratatouille, 192
Rhubarb sauce, 196

S
Safflower dressing with papaya and tarragon, 169–170
Salad dressings and sauces
  Bombay curry sauce, 171–172
  chili mayonnaise, 172
  French olive oil dressing, 170
  fresh tomato piquant, 172
  hazelnut dessing, 169
  herbed hollandaise, 172–173
  horseradish sauce, 173
  peanut dressing, 170–171
  safflower dressing, 169–170
  sesame lemon dressing, 171
  walnut raspberry vinaigrette, 170
Salads
  coleslaw, 194
  Eskimo salad niçoise, 184
Salmon croquettes, 181–182
Salmon in wine, baked, 185–186
Salmon loaf, spiced, 186
Sauces. *See* Salad dressings and sauces
Sesame lemon dressing, 171
Sorbets
  blueberry banana, 200
  ginger pear, 200–201
Soups
  black bean, sherried, 176
  gazpacho, 177–178
  Greek lentil, 177
  split pea and yam, 178-179
  vegetable bean, 179
Spinach fritatta, 188
Split pea and yam soup, 178–179
Substitutions, 208–209
Sweetheart pâté, 175–176

T
Tapioca, 198–199

Tomato piquant, 172
Tuna, grilled, 186–187

V
Vegetable bean soup, 179
Vegetables
    carrots and snow peas,
        minted, 193
    peppers and anchovies, garlic
        roasted, 193

ratatouille, 192
    see also Salads

W
Walnut raspberry vinaigrette, 170

Y
Yam and split pea soup,
    178–179
Yogurt cheese, 141

ABOUT THE AUTHOR

Ann Louise Gittleman, M.S., has an extraordinary background in both traditional nutrition and holistic health. After graduating from Connecticut College, and studying at the New York Institute of Dietetics, she obtained a master's degree in nutrition education from Columbia University.

Since then, she has maintained a private practice for over thirteen years with clients nationwide. Ann Louise served as the Chief Dietitian of the Pediatric Clinic at Bellevue Hospital in New York City, Bilingual Nutritionist for the USDA's Women, Infants, and Children Food Program at a Yale University-connected Health Clinic in New Haven, Connecticut, and as Nutritional Consultant for the first holistic medical group in Connecticut, Deep Brook Associates, which was headed by Dr. John Rhinehart.

Prior to writing her first book, *Beyond Pritikin*, Ann Louise was Nutrition Director at the Pritikin Longevity Center in Santa Monica, California. After leaving the Pritikin Center, she has been a consultant to various nutritionally oriented medical doctors, corporations, and environmental health clinics. She is the chairman of the Department of Nutrition of the American Academy of Nutrition, a member of the American Nutritionists Association, the Holistic Medical Foundation, and the World Research Foundation. She has been a frequent guest on nationwide television and radio and has been interviewed by national newspapers and magazines.

Bantam's Best in Diet, Health and Nutrition

- ❏ 26326-6   ALL-IN-ONE CALORIE COUNTER, Jean Carper $4.95/$5.95 in Canada
- ❏ 25267-4   BRAND-NAME NUTRITION COUNTER, Jean Carper $4.95/$5.95 in Canada
- ❏ 26886-4   COMPLETE SCARSDALE MEDICAL DIET Tarnower and Baker $$4.95/$5.95 in Canada
- ❏ 27775-8   CONTROLLING CHOLESTEROL, Kenneth Cooper, M.D. $5.99/$6.99 in Canada
- ❏ 27667-0   THE ROTATION DIET, Martin Katahn, Ph.D. $4.95/$5.95 in Canada
- ❏ 28508-4   T-FACTOR DIET, Martin Katahn, Ph.D. $5.99/$6.99 in Canada
- ❏ 27751-0   YEAST SYNDROME, Trowbridge, M.D. and Walker $5.95/$6.95 in Canada
- ❏ 34712-8   ASTHMA HANDBOOK, Young and Shulman $9.95/$12.95 in Canada
- ❏ 05771-5   DR. ABRAVANEL'S ANTI-CRAVING WEIGHT LOSS DIET, Elliot Abravanel, M.D. $5.95/$6.95 in Canada
- ❏ 34524-9   THE FOOD PHARMACY, Jean Carper $12.50/$15.50 in Canada
- ❏ 34623-7   HEALING VISUALIZATIONS, Gerald Epstein $8.95/$11.95 in Canada
- ❏ 34618-0   JANE BRODY'S GOOD FOOD BOOK, Jane Brody $15.00/$18.00 in Canada
- ❏ 34721-7   JANE BRODY'S NUTRITION, Jane Brody $15.00/$18.00 in Canada
- ❏ 34350-5   JEAN CARPER'S TOTAL NUTRITION, Jean Carper $12.95/$15.95 in Canada
- ❏ 34556-7   MINDING THE BODY, MENDING THE MIND, Joan Borysenko, M.D. $10.95/$13.95 in Canada
- ❏ 27435-X   THE VITAMIN BOOK, Silverman, M.D., Romano, M.D., Elmer, M.D. $4.95/$6.50 in Canada

■■■■■■■■■■■■■■■■■■■■■■■■■■■■■■■■■■

Available at your local bookstore or use this page to order.

Send to: Bantam Books, Dept. HN
          414 East Golf Road
          Des Plaines, IL 60016

Please send me the items I have checked above. I am enclosing $_____ (please add $2.50 to cover postage and handling). Send check or money order, no cash or C.O.D.'s, please.

Mr/Ms._____

Address_____

City/State_____Zip_____

Please allow four to six weeks for delivery.

Prices and availability subject to change without notice.   HN 12/91

We Deliver!
And So Do These Bestsellers.

☐ 28758-3 **DRIVE: THE STORY OF MY LIFE**
     by Larry Bird $4.95

☐ 27724-3 **TIME FLIES** by Bill Cosby $4.95

☐ 28467-3 **LOVE AND MARRIAGE** by Bill Cosby $4.95

☐ 25660-2 **THE PILL BOOK GUIDE TO**
     SAFE DRUG USE by Harold Silverman $5.50

☐ 27805-3 **TALKING STRAIGHT**
     by Lee Iacocca w/Sonny Kleinfield $5.50

☐ 28057-0 **THE LIVES OF JOHN LENNON**
     by Albert Goldman $5.95

☐ 27601-8 **ULTIMATE EVIL** by Maury Terry $5.95

☐ 34388-2 **800 COCAINE** by Mark S. Gold, M.D. $5.00

☐ 29537-3 **GUINNESS BOOK OF**
     RECORDS 1992 by Norris McWhirter $6.99

☐ 26401-X **MORE HOPE AND HELP FOR YOUR NERVES**
     by Claire Weekes $4.50

☐ 25962-8 **PAUL HARVEY'S THE REST**
     OF THE STORY by Paul Aurandt $4.99

☐ 29927-1 **MOVIES ON TV & VIDEO**
     CASSETTE 1993-1994 by Steven Scheuer $6.99

Buy them at your local bookstore or use this page to order.